Praise for *The Gravity of Up*

"Deep down if you're looking to be set apart, be different, be one of those folks that makes a change, then read *The Gravity of Up* and let Brent take you Up!"

—**JEFF THOMPSON,** executive vice president, Schiavello

"Lots of people have ideas and plans but often lack authenticity. Brent is as real as they come and uses his life story as an example of what it takes to improve the quality of your life. Read *The Gravity of Up* and let Brent show you behind the curtain so you can set your own course for full throttle ahead!"

—**KEVIN HALL,** golf pro, PGA Tour

"Many crumble under the climb for success. *The Gravity of Up* is a humble journey from self-destruction to victory that is both relatable and inspiring. Brent's story provides the keys for success, that if implemented, will propel you to the next level."

—**CHRIS STEPHENS,** senior leader, Northgate Church

"*The Gravity of Up* is a textbook for how to live your life with passion and energy while pursuing excellence! Brent's story proves that you can view hard challenges and obstacles as opportunity to be great. The power of UP is real!"

—**DAVE MCDOWELL,** vice president of development, Athletes in Action

"*The Gravity of Up* shows the power of putting faith in God at all times. Reading the mounting challenges Brent had to overcome has both encouraged me and given me a new level of determination to never give up."

—**STEVEN CADE,** modern country artist

"In *The Gravity of Up*, Brent will show you the importance of being intentional and putting actions behind your words. This book is a lesson in walking the walk and not just talking the talk if you want to have an abundant life. Brent's story is the epitome of that mantra and his results are the proof that it works."

—DR. RICK BRIGGS, owner and director,
Northwest Wellness Center

"*The Gravity of Up* gives you a glimpse into the secret of Brent's massive success. Reliving his story and following his advice to always strive to be more, do more, and give more will lead to success in all facets of life."

—TODD MILLER, friend

"Anyone who picks up *The Gravity of Up* will be inspired by the true story of Brent Yates's up-and-down life. His lessons are endless and his principles will bring happiness and fulfillment to your own life. I have significantly benefited from Brent's journey, his musings, and this book. Now it's your turn."

—TANNER BICKEL, CEO, The
Tanbic Company

"Brent's willingness to show all sides of himself in this book is powerful. His amazing story is relatable to everyone's human struggle, and he shows us all a way out of it. I am honored to call him my friend and excited that the rest of the world gets to know the wisdom he has gained over the years. Anyone who picks up *The Gravity of Up* will be inspired by his story."

—AL FUENTES, mental coach, Al
Fuentes Enterprises

"The best lessons come from people with experience that lead by example. *The Gravity of Up* inspires you to be better and encourages by sharing examples of how it can be done. Brent's words provided me with consistent moments of clarity and a deep awareness of the path I need to pursue if I want more out of life. Read this book and it can do the same for you and your family."
—**JUSTIN FRIED,** CEO, NFI Empire

"*The Gravity of Up* shows us what can be accomplished when you have the desire to be all the Lord wants you to be and when you continue to give yourself to others in need."
—**MAC B. MCELROY**

The Gravity of

UP

UNLOCKING YOUR POTENTIAL
SO NO ONE CAN HOLD YOU DOWN

BRENT YATES

Forefront
BOOKS

Published by Forefront Books.

Print ISBN: 978-1-63763-007-5
E-book ISBN: 978-1-63763-008-2

Cover Design by Bruce Gore, Gore Studio, Inc.
Interior Design by Bill Kersey, KerseyGraphics

Library of Congress Control Number: 2022910859

DEDICATION

*To my beautiful bride, Christina, a true force of
nature and the rock that inspires and fulfills me.
This book is built on your belief in me and
your encouragement to share my journey.*

*Secondly, to all of the people who have come
around and lifted me up and, in turn, trusted
me to pull them along with me: when life
felt heavy, together we experienced a healing
weightlessness. Each and every one of you
came along at the exact moment I needed you,
and now I'm energized about living Up!*

CONTENTS

Foreword 11

Chapter 1: **Chasing the Dream** 13

Chapter 2: **The Power of the Program** 19

Chapter 3: **The Education of Real Life** 37

Chapter 4: **The Battle of the Bond** 49

Chapter 5: **Be Present or Die** 65

Chapter 6: **Waking Up in the Desert** 81

Chapter 7: **A Superhero of Soul** 101

Chapter 8: **Talking at the Man Upstairs** 115

Chapter 9: **Learning to Walk the Walk** 131

Chapter 10: **Striking Out** 149

Chapter 11: **The Setup** 163

Chapter 12: **The Rebuild** 177

Chapter 13: **A Strange Time to Let Go** 189

Chapter 14: **Heading Up!** 205

Acknowledgments 211

About the Author 214

Mental Exercises by Al Fuentes 216

Suggested Reading 221

Reference Notes 221

Notes 222

FOREWORD

I have the honor of writing the Reference foreword to this book—and that's entirely appropriate because, you see, my own relationship with Brent Yates is also just at the beginning. So like you, we will be unfurling this adventure together. I know him now as a successful entrepreneur, devoted father, elated husband, and philanthropist, but I was clueless as to what it took for him to actually get there. His is a story of overcoming. He battled it all—crippling illness, suicidal thoughts, financial ruin, an unfounded lawsuit intent on destroying his name, a nasty divorce, and myriad broken relationships.

As a writer and director, I found it easy to become engrossed with the fascinating autobiographical component of the story that Brent's character plays as the protagonist. However, I invite you to examine yourself as you read through these pages. Don't look at Brent's character as the hero, but look to Brent as the guide. This is the incredible voyage that one man took from death to life and, as you read, you will find pieces of yourself and your own life that connect with Brent's journey. The good news is, you don't have to descend to the depths of his low points to take advantage of what he's gleaned through his growing and healing process. Utilized correctly, this book is less biographical and more tactical. We all have parts of our lives that need healing, and Brent explains how he was able to completely, radically change his life by focusing on three pillars of health—mental, physical, and spiritual.

More than a book, the narrative contained between these covers is meant to be the commencement of a synergistic movement. It's bigger than these pages, and we are all invited to participate. Honestly, the title could have been any number of things: *The Beauty of Up*, *The Power of Up*, *The Adventure of Up*, but, as you will discover, *The Gravity of Up* encompasses all of those aspects. Life *is* a beautiful adventure, and there *is* power in making the decision to move Up. Now, after healing, Brent is ready to use that gravity to change the world. It starts small at first, but he's bringing people along. As the rising tide lifts all ships, this message of positivity and the importance of helping one another will continue to grow this circle wider. Let this book be the beginning of something that makes a difference in your life and your world.

Chris Dowling
Writer/Director

Chapter 1

CHASING THE DREAM

*B*attered knuckles. Bruised, aching legs. The last fumes of adrenaline coursing through my expiring shoulders. This is no leisurely climb up some unassuming mountain. This is total ascension, scaling the vertical cliff wall of El Capitan with no ropes. No safety. Dizzying heights. Defeating gravity.

I want to quit.

But I constantly tell myself to just keep moving Up.

When I thankfully reach my destination at the summit, I celebrate this white-crested peak with a sense of awe and reverence. I amble to the sheer edge and peer back down at the dangerous path I just traversed. The fissures. The crags. The faces.

The faces?

Dreams have a way of revealing our innermost thoughts. Oftentimes, they find the out-of-touch recesses we hide away, and this particular recurring climb dream had plagued me for years. It never made any sense.

Until it did.

The faces etched on these rocks were of every man and woman who had come into my path and breathed life into me when I thought I couldn't go further Up. My immense sense of accomplishment was not mine to own; it was shared with every single one of these people.

Standing atop the apex of this mountain, my feeling of satisfaction is fleeting as I look to my left and spy another mountain, another summit—only this one is higher. Much higher. The challenge becomes clear: "What are you going to do next?"

We typically only think of gravity as the force that holds us down. However, in reality, it's the attraction or pull between all matter. Knowing that, I don't want to be affected by gravity; I want to create it. Metaphorically, of course. As I tackle the next summit and continue to move Up, I want to bring others with me. I want those people to bring others with them . . . and so on and so forth. *Together* is the only way this thing works.

See, Up is not a destination, but a direction.

This crazy journey known as life is built for each and every one of us to achieve greatness, but we won't climb too high trying to go at it alone. Furthermore, if we aren't finding joy in the voyage, we aren't experiencing life itself. It isn't about getting yourself to the top. It's about climbing higher.

I've lived in the valley of despair, gone decades wondering if life were worth living, and questioned if I even had value. The answer is a resounding "yes." However, it took a lifetime for me to figure out how to get there. Now I'm at the place in my life that it's my turn to be the shoulders that elevate others.

I'm not a self-help guru, nor am I trying to become one. I'm simply a guy who lost it all—family, business, finances, even my good name—and then found it again with the help of God, mentors, and people who entered my life with purpose. I was stubborn, selfish, quick to anger, and reeking of human ego. A bomb ready to explode at any time, I kept control by intimidating the ones I worked with—and the ones I loved. The world was something I needed to fight against, and my grind mentality led me to believe that the success I achieved was never enough. Every story has a villain ... and that villain, it turns out, was me. Sound familiar?

From the outside, it looked like I had it all. However, inside I was rotting away and poisoning those around me. It was only when I hit my rock bottom with thoughts of suicide that I decided I was ready to find change. The good news is, it doesn't ever have to get that way for you. Consider this a cautionary tale, but one that proves that life can have a happy ending!

Remember, it doesn't mean this trek is an easy one. There is definitely work to be done in order to make life what you want it. Even with all the support I had, it was still a challenge to open up to new thinking and change programmed behaviors from my past. It took focus and consistency to ignite the transformation in my life. What I learned and experienced during this time of renovation made the difference for me, and I believe it can make a difference for you too.

Remember, together, we are headed Up.

I'm grateful that I was given a second chance at life. I know that phrase can be overexaggerated and banal, but you will come to understand the reason for my over-flowing gratitude. I'm a guy who started in the ditches, welding pipe for my father forty years ago; I ended up the CEO of a booming, multimillion-dollar company with more than 500 employees. My life journey is similar—spiritually, mentally, and physically—finding my way from the personal ditches all the way to the top. Now I'm a committed father, loving husband, doting grandfather, athlete, entrepreneur, and philanthropist.

I have people I deeply love and who love me, a mindset of positivity, and financial abundance that enables me to give back to the causes and organizations that need it most.

My hope is that on your journey to where you want to go, what you want to achieve, and who you want to become, you will take the time to appreciate who you are *now*. Even if you feel stagnant or in limbo, look back and celebrate what you've already overcome. Be thankful to those who have walked away from you and for those who are still with you. And then turn your efforts inward and your vision Up.

Remember, your days are limited, so make them count. Don't think that gravity is only something that holds you down. Our journey begins with the lyrics from one my favorite songs from the band Coldplay:

> *We're going to get it, get it together I know*
> *Going to get it, get it together and flow*
> *Going to get it, get it together and go.*
> *Up and up and up.*[1]

Are you ready to go Up?

Chapter 2

THE POWER OF
THE PROGRAM

*Y*ou are unique. Regardless if you believe that about yourself or not, it is a provable fact. Your life and the routes you've traveled to be where you are at this exact moment in time are distinctive to you. There is no one else on this planet who is exactly like you. Our pathways may all be different, but the one thing we definitely have in common is where we begin: *childhood*.

For some, the term *childhood* conjures thoughts of rainbows, puppies, and a twirling Julie Andrews singing a soundtrack from atop the Austrian Alps. For others, there are no rainbows, no puppies, no Alps—and replace any von Trapp family member with Freddy Krueger and/or Jason because childhood can be scary. Whether fair or not, the majority of our personality is shaped when we are just kids. Essentially, it is the time in our lives when most of our permanent brain programming occurs, affecting our thoughts, feelings, and emotions for the rest of our lives.

Part of the trick of becoming a functioning adult is facing the reality you experienced as a child and interpreting those life experiences through an evolved, healthier lens. It doesn't mean your childhood hasn't affected you (trust me, it has), but it doesn't define you. It is up to you—not your childhood—to decide what you want to make of yourself today. The proof is in the proverbial pudding as time and time again so many kids are given everything as children and do nothing with it as adults. Other children grow up with nothing yet go on to accomplish great things.

When it comes to my own childhood, I don't have that tried-and-true "struggle to greatness" story. However, I'm also not someone who was born with the proverbial silver spoon in my mouth and simply handed everything in life. Like the majority of us, I land somewhere squarely in the middle.

I tell people that I don't remember much of my childhood. I venture to guess it has something to do with getting dropped on my head in middle school. Truthfully, it was less of a drop and more of a hurtling headfirst crash into an oak bookshelf at what felt like 90 miles an hour, courtesy of my buddy Chris Cooper. Sixth graders aren't smart. If you were one or have one, you know this to be true. Chris was no different, and his parents were both at work—a recipe for injury. He convinced me it would be an enjoyable experience to allow him to latch on to both of my legs and violently helicopter spin me as rapidly as he could. He never told me he was going to let go ...

But I could be blocking some things out too.

One of my first memories was from when I was around eight years old. There was a bully, Henry Simpson, picking on me at school. Funny how we forget so much of our childhood, but those moments when we were talked down to, made to feel less than, or were hurt physically or emotionally—those are the memories that cling to us throughout our adulthoods. Even though his name wasn't scary, Henry definitely was. Bigger, stronger, and the first kid on my block to get true facial hair. I never fought back. However, once my parents found out Henry was bullying me, they firmly directed me to stand up for myself and never to back down. It wasn't a suggestion; it was an edict. So the next time Henry gave me a shove after school, I gave him a bloody nose. That was the last day Henry Simpson picked a fight with me. Lesson learned—for both of us.

Now, my prepubescent mind didn't realize it at the time, but I had been allowing Henry to control my life. Even when he wasn't physically near me, he occupied coveted space inside my head as I was constantly worrying about running into him on the street or seeing him at recess. Think about it. You probably have a Henry Simpson or two in your own life. Of course, I'm not talking about an actual third grade bruiser, but there probably is somebody who's stealing your "gravity of Up." These are the people who weigh you down and cause negativity in your life. As we move forward, let me be clear that the childhood lesson I learned is just as true for you as it was for me: *no one can hold you down!*

Now, I chose to own that mindset and even take it a step further by never backing down from that point on. By the time I was in high school, I was willing to go head-to-head with anyone who gave me a hard time (sometimes even a *medium* time). It wasn't a whole lot of physical fighting, but it didn't have to be, as the other kids recognized not to mess with me. I liked that feeling. In fact, I craved it, and that hardened, never-back-down attitude (for good but mostly for bad) shaped the next thirty years of my life. That mindset had me believe there was only one way to win and that was to fight against any resistance. Now I can look back and see that many times, it was only perceived resistance in my path or friction that I was creating just for the thrill of the fight. Nine times out of ten, I was my own problem.

Does that sound familiar in your own life? At some point, I shifted from an external presence stealing my gravity to becoming my own worst enemy. Strangely, I became the person holding myself down. If that's where you are at right now, I assure you that together we will break those chains and get you positioned to head Up. As you go on this journey with me, I'll show you how to navigate the rough waters so you can find your healthy promised land. Trust me, I know it's not an easy or simple process, but I know because I've been there and have found joy on the other side! It's all about recognizing what is not working in your life so you can fix it. As I said, most of those negative patterns begin in our adolescence.

Win-at-all-costs fighting wasn't the only programming I learned as a child. I have vague memories of being ten years old and hanging out at my dad, Gene's, shop—Mid-Ohio Pipeline (MOP), a company he independently started in 1970. I remember all the hulking machinery, the tools, and the guys. It was completely fascinating to me. What little kid wouldn't want to be surrounded by all that enchanting equipment? Running a small business kept Dad away from the house for most days and plenty of nights. If I wanted to spend time with my father, I had to meet him where he was at—both physically and emotionally. This would become a pattern I found myself repeating as I got older and had a family of my own. In order to be close to me, my loved ones needed to fit into my world, not the other way around. Fifty years later, I can still vividly remember going to Dad's shop, knowing that was the best way to connect with him.

As I got older, my desire to be a part of my dad's routine progressed to aspirations of wanting to be a part of his company. So at the age of fourteen, I spent my summer officially working in the family business. The days really were long as we would leave before sunrise at 5 a.m. and wouldn't get back home until that giant flaming ball had gone to sleep. I would do any job my old man allowed, including digging holes, spotting utilities, jackhammering asphalt, padding pipe, throwing concrete, and moving gravel. At MOP, every employee did every job, and that is exactly how my dad wanted it. He felt that if everyone knew how to properly pull off each task, then when someone missed a day we could keep going without slowing down. That wasn't easy to do as a kid, but I wanted my dad to see me as one of his guys with no excuses and no complaints.

Now, I didn't work every single day in the summer. I still played sports, went to camps, and took occasional days off to just be a kid. Between toiling at the shop in the summers and excelling at sports in school, I was shaping my mind to compete and win at all costs. This mentality can put a burdensome load of preteen pressure on a young man, but I did have the support of my mom and dad. To be honest, much of the time it felt like too much support; I began feeling as if I weren't the only one applying pressure on myself to be the best.

On the evenings when my father made it home from work on time, dinnertime at the kitchen table was where my parents and I would convene to talk and recap our day. Primarily the discussions revolved around Dad's business: how it was going and how it could be better. When we were not talking all things MOP, sports became the focus. Mom and Dad would surgically go through my games and evaluate my performances with a laser focus. They were quick to inform me how I could be better with precise prescriptions how to fix any on-court shortcomings. While their intentions were pure, it was a lot for me to handle. I began looking less forward to dinner discussions until it got to the point where I was actually dreading that roundtable. Looking back, I believe this is where I began shutting down communication-wise.

I had little desire to relentlessly talk about how to get better at business, sports, and school all the time. Sometimes I just needed a bite of meatloaf and a laugh or for someone to simply ask me how my day was without any expectations. Again, my parents truly meant no harm, but they were unrealized victims of their own childhood programming. They were driven and more accustomed to doing the talking rather than the listening. At times, our meals were a competition to see who could in get more words or advice before dad's post-dinner coffee. Eventually, I would silently ruminate on how much I didn't want to talk while the conversation blistered around me. Before I knew it, I became a man of few words and poor communication. I excelled at hiding my emotions behind a smile or agreeable nod.

My mom, JoAnn, was not only a formidable force inside our family, but in life as a whole. To this day, at eighty-three years old, she is still ballroom dancing and taking the world by storm. She was always the kind of woman who could back down any man and that, unfortunately, included my father. She was an amazing athlete who would overwhelm anyone in her path by an imposing strength in her voice—and actions. I have always respected her. She still is truly the only person whom I believe I have never been able to intimidate. No matter how hard I tried. Not even a little bit. Trust me.

When my dad came home from an exhausting day at the shop, she would strategize with him—whether he wanted to or not—asking questions and peppering him with her fiery opinions as to how to grow the business. Mom was always trying to help him succeed and would often ask, "What about this idea, Gene?" She was the astute keeper of the company's books and knew how every penny was spent, saved, or wasted. No one had a better handle on MOP's financials, and she strived to make the company operate more efficiently. Truthfully, it was a blessing that she was on top of the books because the shop was stretched to full capacity. There was very little cash, if any at all, to spare.

There was always an intense energy at the dining room table. By dinner, Dad was ready to decompress from the day, but he seldom got that reprieve. It wasn't because anything was wrong between my parents; it was just the nature of my father's business and the industry as a whole. Daily, lives were at stake and the margins ran so tight that one slight mishap could shut down the entire company for good. My father operated under that unbearable tension every day of his working life. Family and business can certainly make for strange bedfellows.

Dealing with energy pipelines is dangerous. Literally, it was a life-and-death venture of inches, not feet. Imagine welding a new line into an existing live natural gas line amidst 8-ton backhoes and other cumbersome construction equipment constantly shifting around you while you are cutting. The earthquaking clatter of jackhammers and a dozen other pieces of equipment is reverberating in your hard hat so loudly that you can't hear yourself think, much less concentrate on the potentially lethal task at hand.

One wrong move from a preoccupied employee can kill everyone on a jobsite. Living this intense craziness as a child for so long, I found myself even as an adult struggling to physically relax or let my guard down. In fact, I truly believe that this armored, protective mindset leaked over into my life and, ultimately, my relationships.

Despite all of this stress, my dad was a loving guy known to be a compelling leader at his business and in the community. Unfortunately, that leadership did not extend to the marriage. My mother dominated that arena. I will never know if my dad was simply so tired from life that he deferred to her or if she usurped the power early on. Either way, my mom told my dad how everything was going to be, and she stood by it. She laid out how he was going to act, what he was going to wear, when he was going to schedule his annual health appointments, even what he was going to eat (or not eat). In my mother's eyes, my father could *never* do anything right, even as his business grew. No matter what he achieved, it still was never enough, and I can still her voice today saying, "Gene, you can't do that!"

Now, the point here is not to paint a bad picture of my mother. However, if you don't break programming cycles, you will just repeat them. My mother stepped into their marriage the same way that her mother did, and I can only assume her mother before that. They are a line of strong and assertive women. There are plenty of advantages that come from having a strong mother in your life, but you learn quickly to toe the line or be dealt with harshly. As a young boy, experiencing the way my mom controlled my dad and the household impacted me greatly and would affect my own future marriage in a tragic way.

However, at that time, I was just a kid living life, and she was just a mom trying her best to raise a young man. Upon further reflection, it was the start of my fierce opposition to listening to anyone else's advice, comments, or concerns. "My way or the highway" quickly became my mantra, as cliché as that may sound. As I got older, I would continually take that idea to new heights and wear it like a badge of honor.

It is only now, as a healthy adult, that I'm able to go back willingly to observe my life without judgment. I have allowed myself to see how I was programmed based on my interpretation of life and experience. *Interpretation* is the key noun here, as the process is built upon three major components: a message, a giver, and a receiver. Without the learned dynamic of clear communication, there is so much that can go wrong in that transaction. Once it falters from the onset, bad communication has the ability to fester and build until the relationship implodes. When you are prepared, you can look over ruined friendships and identify how the cratering began with a stupid, ill-communicated inter-pretation. This was something I had to learn the hard way and do the work to reprogram myself, but I'm not there—yet!

By the time I was a senior in high school, I was getting up early and heading out of the house without speaking a word to anyone. I wouldn't even let my mom make me breakfast as I didn't want to open myself up to any chance of dialogue or conversation. My mother was still trying to love me the best way she knew, but she couldn't recognize how much I was actually closing down. As I got older, I learned to subtly stand up for myself in less abrasive ways against my mom's constant coaching and advice. In a peculiar sense, I believe the more resolute I became, the more respect she gave me. I wish I had seen my father standing up for himself in the same way.

Around the time I was gaining independence from my mom, I also needed to release any tethers to my father. I wanted to become my own man. I don't think that desire is unusual by any means, and for most fifteen-year-old boys it's a completely acceptable rite of passage. However, as with all things, I chose to push it to the next level. With a distorted view, I began regarding my father as my competition. The same as it was with anyone I saw as a competitor, it was his responsibility to get out of my path or be destroyed.

It all started with a Christmas gift.

I asked my parents for an Atari 2600 and a Farrah Fawcett poster, but instead I got two sets of boxing gloves.

Two sets? The message was clear. This was not simply for some exercise and shadowboxing; this was meant for actually pounding on another person. I am sure in some way it was my parents' idea to support my "stand up for yourself" approach to life. So like any pubescent entrepreneur, I set up boxing matches in my backyard with friends. We didn't have a glorious belt to fight for, but we did have baseball cards and lunch money for the winners. Somewhere along the way, I must have thought I had gotten pretty dang good, because I got the crazy idea that I could take my old man.

Despite my persistent pestering, Dad never took me up on my sanctioned offer of five rounds in the backyard. However, one day in a totally non-pugilist conversation, I agitated this gentle giant just enough that he casually obliged. "Why don't you go get those boxing gloves and let's go downstairs," he said. I didn't even hesitate. In fact, I vaguely remember being pretty excited about it.

With heightened swagger, down those dusty stairs to the basement we went. There was no fancy James Brown "Living in America" *Rocky IV* entrance music to lead us into the ring, no baseball card–victory purse, nor even a backyard crowd to entertain. It was just my old man, my Christmas boxing gloves, and me. He may have had the reach and the weight advantage with biceps as big my thighs, but I had speed and what I thought was skill. One thing I'm certain I did not lack was confidence. I liked my odds.

I don't remember what prefight words were said or even if I got a single punch off. All I remember is his gruff, "Go!" and then staring up at him from somewhere deep inside the fireplace (fortunately there were no logs...or fire). It was a one-punch thing, or so I was told, that dropped me backward so hard that I was now located among the blackened ash. Was it poetic justice or mere coincidence? Either way, the chimney was the perfect landing place because my ego got smoked.

Twenty-twenty hindsight. It was beneficial for me to experience that moment because it helped put me in check...somewhat. If we are open and attuned to them, humbling experiences can really bring a positive reset of perspective. I was still too naive and drinking my own Kool-Aid to take any larger life lessons from my beatdown at the time, but that was the final invitation I ever gave my old man to put on the gloves. Nevertheless, the fight inside of me to get ahead of him remained, and truth be told, it was probably just getting stoked. I never literally went toe-to-toe with my dad on a physical level again, but I would find other ways to come out on top.

In his own way, my dad pushed me in the right direction. Not all the stress he put on my plate was bad. He ingrained in me at an early age the power of hard work and the yearning to be the best. Part of that mindset, whether I liked it or not (and I initially did not), was his insistence that I was going to college to get educated so I could take over the family business. There was no second-guessing or altering this plan as he had put that bug in my ear when I was as young as five years old. What began as nudges in my youth converted to full-on shoves by my teens as my dad constantly told me, "You will take over our family company and you will take care of us." That was an immense amount of pressure to place squarely on the shoulders of a pimply kid who was an entirely average student in school.

As I matured, I realized that dreams other than running MOP were materializing for me. More than anything, I wanted to be a stuntman in the movies. That's right. With my love for fast cars and notable athleticism, this Ohio boy became certain that an escape to Hollywood was exactly what I needed for the next phase in my life. As graduation got closer, I played the conversation countless times over and over in my scrambled brain—telling my father that I was going to forgo the family business and head to the West Coast to take falls, throw punches, and race sports cars.

Whether it was fear of the unknown or fear of my old man, with summer approaching things suddenly started to shift. I thought endlessly about *my father's* goals for me, and I ultimately decided to pursue what he would deem "the responsible path." I buried my dreams of Hollywood excitement and adventure somewhere deep inside of me and enrolled in college. I specifically remember the gut-punch feeling of sidelining my own dreams to put others' expectations ahead of my own happiness. This would prove to be a recurring theme throughout my life.

I told myself that this was what being a leader was about—sacrifice. I was still too young and too poorly programmed to see the value of balance in life. I had to learn, decades later, to recognize that true leadership is finding the place where my own expectations and desires coincide with the expectations and needs of others around me. You can't lead from a place of fear. The opposite of fear is not calm or peace. The opposite of fear is faith. To be a leader, you must have faith in yourself—and, I believe, faith in God (but more on that later). Fear believes lies we've been told by others and the ones we tell ourselves. True faith armors your mindset to protect you from lies, doubt, and fear.

Being a leader comes with an inventory of responsibilities that aren't always pleasant or desired. Despite all of our challenges, I knew I still had so much to ascertain from my old man as a mentor and occupational role model. In life and business, there are natural-born leaders and there are leaders who learn how to step into that role. I am the latter, but I had the best to push me. I was without a doubt 100 percent molded by my father's example, and we shared the same pathos—hard work, competition, and victory.

However, he didn't realize that I still viewed him as a rival—a measuring stick that I had to rise above. As I got older and my life became an out-of-control scorched earth of success at all costs, I found that I, sadly, had left my old man in the burn.

My father's steadfast belief in me was so compelling that it triggered me to believe in myself, even as I had those coming-of-age doubts that plague us all. He saw me bigger than I viewed myself and looked past where I was to envision the heights I could reach down the road. I would still have to choose self-confidence, but how he regarded me was a vigorous self-fulfilling prophecy that pushed me to excel. Dad's powerful certainty in others was a leadership trait that I observed throughout his life and did my best to replicate in my own journey with MOP.

Michael Jordan is the greatest player to ever play the game of NBA basketball. You can dispute it and throw out other vaunted names such as Magic, Kobe, Wilt, or LeBron, but you can also be very wrong. The thing that made Jordan supreme wasn't his ten scoring titles or fourteen NBA All-Star selections. It wasn't even that his *Space Jam* was monumentally better than LeBron's reboot. What made His Airness legendary had much less to do with *I* and everything to do with *team*.

His Chicago Bulls team was perfect 6-0 in the NBA Finals and consistently had the best record in regular season basketball. The secret (maybe not so secret) to Jordan's success as a leader was that he made every player around him better. He had vision—not just for himself, but vision for the entire team on the court—coupled with the innate ability to motivate and get the best out of people. In some strange way, I think my dad had a little bit of Jordan in him (in the workshop, but definitely not on the court). Maybe he saw me as his Scotty Pippen, and even though I wasn't quite ready to fully realize my potential, I was headed in the right direction.

However, there was a yearning inside me that felt like I wasn't living life for myself anymore. That is a scary place to find yourself and certainly is not unique to my situation. Most of us find ourselves in that confusing territory from time to time. Let me be clear: that feeling does not have to last for a lifetime. It is temporal, and you can break through it. I know this for a fact because I certainly did. It's not necessarily easy, but it is worth it.

You'll see for yourself as I walk through my recovery in the pages of this book.

It is not what you do that makes you who you are; it is how you show up in what you do that defines you. Even if you feel worthless or powerless, you have value because the One who created the world, created you specifically. That value is intrinsic and no person or thing can ever strip it from you. Ever hear people brag about being "one in a million"? Well, in a world of 7.8 billion people that means there are 7,800 other people just like you. The reality is that you are far more special than that, and there is literally no one on this planet exactly like you. That's the truth.

You are one in a universe.

Chapter 3

THE EDUCATION
OF REAL LIFE

*W*ith graduation behind me, I was off to Ohio Northern University in Ada, Ohio. The only stunts I would perform for the next two years were on the basketball court. I was an invited as a walk-on shooting guard, and the head coach guaranteed me a spot on the squad. I would play ball and compete with everyone else, but I always felt like an outsider since I wasn't a scholarship player. After being the big man on campus in high school where sports, girls, and popularity came easily, this was a new and troubling feeling. Looking back, I see this as another lesson in the making. As I grew older, I developed great empathy for those who are considered "outsiders," or as the Bible coins them, "the least of these." Of course, my college situation was first world problems, and there are true outsiders struggling with daily life. Today I have a heart for hurting people and use my charities to help lift them up above their burdens.

One thing feeling displaced did was fuel my competitive nature. Even though I did everything to make college and hoops work, they simply weren't enough to hold my interest. Maybe it was the latent Hollywood bug still residing in my heart, but I decided I was done with Ohio Northern University and any type of a formal college education after one and a half years.

A business degree seemed like a necessary evil that I was getting just to please my father. I knew the family company would eventually be handed over to me, and I fully realized it would be *helpful* to have a business degree under my belt, but I wasn't convinced it was "necessary." I was a business major, and my professors were preaching the range of a $30,000 starting salary once I hit the marketplace with a degree. That wasn't bad money back then; most of my class seemed genuinely excited about the prospects of that kind of dough, but I wanted more. I knew I could make more than my peers by simply going back home and working for my dad. There is something to be said about earning a degree and getting that magical piece of paper, but sometimes there is more to be gained from a trial by fire. Schooling oftentimes gives us the theory, but the flames give us the experience and mechanism. I knew which path was right for my situation, so I packed my bags and headed back to Pendleton.

If I were going to be forged by the fire, it was time to get serious about the family business and learn more about the actual trade. My old man knew where he wanted me to start at MOP—the bottom! I was definitely not the prodigal son returning home and being given the best robe, ring, and fancy sandals by his overjoyed father. There was no "fatted calf" for the big return feast; there was only me unceremoniously signing up for a ten-day welding course at a school in Oklahoma.

However, what my father did was the difference in me passing my final test and failing. He would complete his sixty-hour workweek at MOP and then teach me hands-on welding skills on the weekends. Under his tutelage, I passed the exam. His lessons were more valuable than anything I learned during my course. These are fond memories, as it was one of the few times that I remember actively listening to direction from my father.

Going home not only meant getting back to the family business, it also meant being near my girlfriend. During the summer between my freshman and sophomore years of college, I had met a girl who was a senior at my old high school. She was strikingly beautiful and our dating was fast and furious. Like many first loves, we could do no wrong, and we couldn't get enough of each other. Just one year later, we were married.

By this time, I was fully invested in MOP and putting in countless hours at the shop and on the jobsites. My relentless work schedule was a challenge for my marriage, but it definitely wasn't the biggest issue. My childhood programming really showed up in an unexpected way. I truly desired to be in an equal partnership where both my wife and I had opinions, feelings, and ideas that were worthy of discussion, but after watching my mother wear the pants in my parents' marriage, I quickly demonstrated that I didn't want anyone telling me what to do or how to live my life.

I decided that my wife couldn't tell me anything—nothing. I was not going to listen to her, take orders from her, or be spoken to in the manner that my mom spoke to my dad. No one was going to tell me how to act, what to wear, or what to eat. My voice would be the final word. Every time. This type of closed-minded thinking rarely leads to living your greatest life or developing a healthy marriage, but amazingly as humans, we still try to control everything. There is no relationship where there is no communication.

In trying to distance myself from the broken dynamics of my parents' marriage, I was basically repeating their relationship. Unfortunately, this time I was the one playing the role of dictator to my wife in the same way that my mother lorded over my father. As you can imagine, that did not create good communication or feelings of safety and understanding within my marriage. Even though our relationship was crumbling throughout the early years of our marriage, we still played family and had three beautiful children—our son, Jordan, and our daughters Lauren and Krista.

By the time I was twenty-nine, I realized I was sleeping, eating, and living with a woman who didn't like me, and, truth be told, I didn't like her. We hadn't simply grown apart; we had pushed each other apart. Typically, it was conscious actions that we did to hurt each other, but also to blame was much of our unrecognized childhood programming that flew under the radar. I didn't want to hurt our kids by getting divorced, so I remained in our unhappy union.

Looking back, I have to wonder: if we'd divorced earlier, would our kids have been happier overall? Would they have had less stress and tension in a home without two unhappy parents? How much did we negatively program them by staying together? There is no way to ever answer these questions, but I have faith that things happen for a reason.

Let's be clear—no one ever plans to get married just to get a divorce. Never have I attended a wedding where the pastor said, "Do you promise to stay by each other's sides through good times and bad, for richer or poorer, in sickness and health? Do you vow to stay true and love unconditionally 'til . . . two years or so? Maybe three, give or take? Then we can circle back and see if we wanna re-up this whole thing for another two years?"

Of course not, it's *'til death do us part* for a reason. So we all start with the right intentions, but just like so many things in life, marriage can so easily go off-track. Unless both people are dedicated to working on a relationship to fix the broken parts, it is hard to maintain a working marriage. However, I thought I was doing the best that I could with what I knew at the time.

I was living with my childhood programming and serving the loop of my own ego. If you judge yourself in hindsight, you will not see the gifts that allowed you to develop and flourish. People usually don't want to look back because of that nasty feeling of regret. If you can reflect without guilt or shame and know that God works good out of all things, then you can see the lessons you learned that altered your path. Once healthy, you can map those moments and cherish the realization that, without them, you would have never had the knowledge and courage to catapult Up.

My marriage was not the only place of mounting friction in my life. My father and I had numerous similarities, but it was our differences concerning the business that were really defining our relationship. Cracks were splintering and growing in size—more than I would like to admit. The irony of my father molding me to be an alpha leader from such a young age is that I struggled to follow anyone, including him.

With only two years of college behind me, I strangely represented the more educated part of our family business. Conversely, my father embodied the worker and craftsman side of the business. Where he was built to lower his head and plow through grinding work day after day, I was built to strategize a clear path to victory regardless of what that looked like, whom I pissed off, and whom I pushed out of the way. My competitive appetite was the fuel that drove me out of control. It's a good thing I didn't have a brother because, at that point in my life, I would have killed him just to get him out of my way. Some real Cain and Abel stuff—that's how serious it would have become.

My father grew up during the Great Depression, which influenced him to be conservative and risk-averse, but I wanted to fly without a safety net to generate revenue as fast as possible. I was a gambler, and my philosophy was, "Let's grow it! Let's roll!" On blazing fire, I was absolutely convinced that I was not only going to set every sales record at the company, but in the industry as a whole.

I would bounce novel ideas off my dad, and the majority of the time I would get a stern, "Are you crazy? We can't do that!" Two years into my tenure at MOP, I was fed up with my father's negative feedback to my increasingly grandiose ideas. I finally shouted at him, "I don't need you. You grew me to be this way." I never thought about what that must have felt like for my old man to hear his son say the words *I don't need you.* As a father and grandfather, all I can say is that I hope I never repeat that moment with my children or grandchildren. And the truth was, I did need my dad—even if my ego didn't let me realize it at the time.

It gets worse. The tipping point in our relationship came a few years later. When he was in his forties, Dad would shut the whole business down in the wintertime and spend the colder months in Florida with the family. Winters in Ohio are typically harsh, and the bitter conditions take their toll on both men and machines digging into the frozen earth. I fashioned myself a visionary who foresaw the need to work year-round if the business was ever going to grow. At that time, I had mistakenly entrenched my value as a person based upon the profits of the company. My father was trying to teach me balance with his lifestyle choices, but I was rocketing ahead with only one thought: success. I was as dead set on having my way of a year-round business as my dad was on keeping our operations exactly the same. Eventually, I wrote him off, "You go do your thing, and I'm going to do my thing," I told him.

That is exactly what we did.

For a long time, I harbored regrets over those strange years. Dad and I did not have a decent relationship because I still had zero desire to listen to anybody, including him, my business partner and parent. On top of that, I had allowed a huge swell of resentment to build up over the years.

Even though he was physically the strongest man I knew, with infamous one-punch-knockout power, I viewed his role in his marriage as a weakness. I did not have time for the weak, especially with regard to running our company. By then, Dad had become the one obstacle to me taking full charge of the family business.

Instead of honoring him as my father, mentor, and the man who started the company, I was annoyed he was still at work each day trying to tell me what to do, trying to direct my life and my future.

All my ideas to grow MOP felt too risky for my father. My wife seemed to agree. However, where my mother was entirely invested in the family business, my wife didn't have the same interest. Being a homemaker and taking care of our children were her primary focus, and I applaud her for that choice. When I did try to include her in the business discussions, she would have strong opinions without having all the facts. Nothing would exasperate me more, and the decisions I made were typically opposite of what she recommended. Truth be told, I was never really looking for her honest thoughts; I only wanted confirmation that my ideas were right. With each piece of her dissenting commentary on my business directives, I found myself shutting down more and more.

Can you see how resentment deeply rooted in the belief that my life was not my own had infiltrated and infected my life?

I wanted my dad to think I knew everything and, to be honest, I probably wanted my wife to think that too. I truly craved for him to be proud of me, but I had no way to convey that since we were not a family of meaningful words or heartfelt conversations. Looking back, I wish I had known how to express myself better to him. I know many of the things I did say cut him badly enough to leave permanent emotional scars. However, I had yet to learn any healthy, crucial communication skills.

I had already been running the day-to-day operations for a couple of years, but I officially took over as president of MOP in 1996 when I was thirty-six years old. The day I formally cemented my title, I paid my father cash for the book value of our company. He signed over the stock to me, and I wrote the check to him. It was with a not-so-graceful, impersonal fashion that I pushed him out of the company he had started twenty-six years earlier.

I don't think either of us felt good about the exchange, but I just wanted him to walk away so I could implement my forward-thinking ways. While he and Mom were able to buy a house in Florida with the money from the sale, I allowed him to stay on as a consultant for a few more years. I could see that he wasn't quite ready to let go of work just yet, and I did my best to honor his feelings. He was still very skilled with the hands-on operations in the shop, but I did not allow him in the field any longer.

Eventually, even his presence in the shop became tiresome, so in 1999 I gave him a gold ring to signal his complete retirement from the company and the end of his machine shop visits. Looking back, I see how far away I was from kindness and compassion, as Dad must have felt gutted by his own flesh and blood for pushing him out of his beloved business.

Freed from work, Dad now had plenty of time to spend with family and discovered great enjoyment being a grandfather. Meanwhile, I was spending every waking moment building the business, and it became the whole "Cat's in the Cradle" thing as I didn't have time to sit around, talk, and strengthen our father-son relationship. Now that I was at the helm, if I wanted to grow MOP exponentially, it meant working days, nights, and weekends.

As time marched on and higher revenues trickled in, I wanted recognition from Dad and everyone else for all the hard work, hours, and sweat equity I had put into taking MOP to the next level. All Dad wanted was to reconnect with his son. As he had grown older, he realized the error of his ways during my childhood and wanted to fix our relationship. Wisdom that comes with age had really refined what was important to my father, and it sure wasn't toiling your life away while your family suffers.

As I look back without judgment, I wish I had learned my father's lesson much earlier in life. Even today, reflecting on the paradigm of what I think is important motivates me to strive to better myself even when it's uncomfortable. However, even with all the work I have done on myself, I recognize that I am still a work in progress. I spoke about having regrets at the time, but now I know differently. It's imperative that you do something about any pain from your past. Figure out why you showed up the way you did at the time and evaluate what you would have done differently. Then change your programming so that you can live in that manner now.

That is how you change your regret into a gift!

Chapter 4

THE BATTLE OF THE BOND

*I*n 2000, MOP was headquartered out of one location but we operated at numerous jobsites throughout Ohio. We were humming along and consistently turning $3 to $4 million a year in revenue. I was basking in the success, but still never settling. Allowing myself to be content was not an option with the trajectory of my business. We were bulletproof, and nothing could slow us down.

Then everything changed.

It all started when Columbia Gas of Ohio, our biggest customer, began dictating rates and made contractual changes that left it nearly impossible for us to continue to turn a profit. As soon as their tactics became evident, I had a very clear decision to make. This was my David vs. Goliath moment, and if I didn't take a stand for my company, Columbia Gas would just keep driving down prices until we literally could no longer make the margins work. MOP would go broke.

Now, understand that taking a stand meant telling our largest client, which made up 95 percent of our receipts, that we were no longer going to work with it. This would be a monumental risk and a vast leap of faith, not only in myself, but also in MOP. I'm a fighter who didn't see any other way to move forward, so I took my stand. I informed Columbia Gas that we would no longer be doing business with it. The only option I had to keep my business up and running was to try to break into the public sector of the water and sewer market using our gas line equipment.

In the public works market, your work has to be bonded. That more or less means the company and my personal assets financially guarantee the work will be completed to a project's specifications. If I were competing for a $3 million job and MOP was only worth $2 to $3 million, I would literally be gambling everything on that one job. With ever-shifting factors beyond our control, a thousand things could go wrong, such as weather or supply issues, delayed late start dates, substandard materials, employee injuries, and so on.

Also, for the first time in my career, outsiders were now looking into my business practices and financial statements. Banks and bonding companies evaluated MOP every time we took out a bond. It was unnerving to know that I'd always have someone looking over my shoulder. The pressure was immense . . . and building.

With so little company equity, getting bonded became very personal as I had no other choice but to put my house on the line. If something happened and the company couldn't pay what was owed, the bondholder could take everything from me. Now, that meant my family's house as well.

It was a frightening process, but sometimes in the trepidation God throws us breadcrumbs. I found peace and a small silver lining that during the approval process, the bonding companies consistently spoke highly about the strength of MOP. Hearing an outsider's praise and validation proved to me that we were successful. As I've established, at this point in my life and career, I was constantly seeking approval to feed my ego.

Our prospective customers must have felt the same way as the bank did about us because once we were ready to go, we had no trouble getting bonded work. With every new gig, my conviction edged closer to hubris that I had made the right call to dump Columbia Gas. By dropping the lifeline we had relied on for decades, we were pushed to find new places to grow. The boom in new accounts was confirmation that we were doing something very right at MOP.

In business, it is paramount to find the balance between you and the customer. That relationship is meant to be a give-and-take both ways. When it slides out of balance in your favor, the customer will let you know in some way, shape, or form. Trust me. If the customer is taking too much, you have to take a stand. It can be paralyzing, but you have to protect your business and your employees. Sometimes you just have to bet on yourself.

You can see how so many of the lessons I've learned in my line of work are actually bigger than business. How could using that same mentality of balancing the give-and-take in our personal relationships affect our lives? Would your life be any different if you recognized bad relationships and took a stand when needed to protect yourself and the ones you love? Are you able to look around you and identify those who are trying to hold you down?

The risk definitely increased significantly, but the financial reward did as well. The new strategy I implemented skyrocketed MOP to annual revenues of $14 to $16 million practically overnight. For my efforts, I was nominated for an Ernst & Young Entrepreneur of the Year award.

Sadly, while the company was doing better than ever, the hours and stress partnered with a crumbling marriage were about to throw me another awful curveball.

I remember the first signs of the illness. I was sitting in my office when our VP, Tom Lorenz, walked in to hand me some meaningless paperwork. It was 4:00 p.m., but the day was far from being over. I'd spent several hours in meetings, reviewing numbers, and making decisions, but there was more work to be done. The truth is, there was always more work to be done and not enough hours in the day to do it.

At forty-three, I had been at MOP full-time for twenty-three years. Since I had taken over, eighty-hour workweeks and high stress were my norm. I was never able to put work out of my mind, so I rarely took a break to relax, unwind, or spend time with my family. This nonstop pace was all I knew because it was all I'd ever seen from my dad. And, I didn't want to be *as* successful as him—I needed to be *more* successful than him.

As soon as I reached out to take Tom's paperwork, my stomach turned and tightened. A brutal wave of pain quickly shot through my abdomen. It was definitely something I hadn't felt before, but I blew it off as some bad Thai food from lunch. Besides, I definitely didn't have time to be ill. I soon forgot about the pain as I lost myself in several more hours of emails and phone calls.

The very next day, the pain was back—and more intense—impossible to blame on the Pad Thai. This time there was a lasting, deep, burning sensation that really scared me. It wasn't just uncomfortable; it was a legitimate, searing pain. I still didn't know what was wrong, but I knew whatever it was, it wasn't good. Tom recommended that I take a couple of days off. That sounded like an insane proposition to me.

Instantly, I thought about my business and how everything was leveraged at that point in time, including *me*. I was working as many hours as humanly possible, and it was totally embedded in my mind that I had to keep up this pace or it could all fall apart. Everything about my identity was chained to my work and proving my worth. It shouldn't take debilitating physical pain to bring me to a place of proactive change, but looking back, I'd like to think that God knew that was the only way I would be open to it. It wasn't until my body started breaking down that I considered there could be another way to live my daily life. It was evident that work was my poison.

How many times does it take for immense pain to finally push us into action? The pain could be physical, emotional, or spiritual, but so often it has to hurt enough to bring us to our knees to make us ready to embrace change. How much better could life be if we were open and available enough to cut off the things that give us agony before it gets to that point? It's important to recognize the poisons in our lives before they make us too sick to move Up.

I quickly realized that if I went down for any extended time with this illness or the next one, our company was not going to survive. It was time to hire some like-minded, high-level people around me to whom I could delegate the work. As someone who was always in control and on top, this was a menacing wager. Not only was I nervous about handing over some responsibilities, but there were bigger questions: *Could I afford them? Could I find enough new business to cover the costs? Would they fit into our familial atmosphere?* I was still operating with the mindset that the bottom line should not be to preserve my health, but to preserve the health of my company.

The next day, I immediately thought of two business associates who had great integrity and work ethics. I recognized they had the qualities that would make them great employees, but neither of them had a background in the pipeline business. However, these men had something more important than industry experience—they had earned my trust over the years. They had the character and intangibles to fit the ethos of my family's company, so I hired them knowing they would help take the burden off me—both physically and mentally.

Even though hiring people is still tremendously difficult for me, I soon recognized how the new members of the team spurred the business to grow. I surrounded myself with more new hires who caught my vision, and the new blood brought a wave of new energy. I found myself fired up to secure more accounts, even though I was trying to peel back on my weekly hours. No longer wanting to be a one-man show, I knew I had to operate differently and continue to surround myself with the right people to truly achieve the success I wanted for MOP. With that emerging awareness, I started to consider the fractured relationships in my personal life.

In 2000, the same year I had the strange stomach pains, Dad had a stroke. I knew my old man was tough as hell, but when I heard the diagnosis, the first thought that raced through my head was, *He's not going to make it.* Isn't it puzzling that we almost always immediately jump to the negative? There is something so human about fear. It's understandable to worry, but to instantly believe the worst-case scenario never helps a situation. Fear removes your ability to be in the present even though it is entirely based on something that *might* happen in the future. In fact, I'm willing to bet that 95 percent of the things that cause us worry and fear never materialize. All that worry strips away our present joy for a future that may never exist. This case was no different as my initial worry turned out to be completely wrong. My old man made a full recovery.

That ordeal changed my father, and his demeanor shifted after the stroke. He became gentler, almost fragile, in my perspective. Looking back, I think he was simply grateful for the time he had left and realized he just wanted to be around those he loved. I wish I had made more of an effort to spend time with him, but I was still a workaholic with little time for relationship building—or healing, in our case. Also, no matter how frail I watched him get, there is a part of every man that will always see a piece of his father as being invincible. I probably tricked myself into believing that *invincible* meant *immortal* and that somehow he would always be around. Now that he'd fully recovered from the stroke, in my mind nothing could take him out. He would live forever, and maybe one day we'd get our stuff together for eighteen holes and reminisce about the good life we'd built. In the meantime, I had to keep building and advancing my MOP empire.

Four years after his stroke, a body scan indicated a small mass in my father's lungs. It had gone undetected, which allowed it to continue to grow unabated. When the medical staff did finally catch it, Dad was diagnosed with stage IV lung cancer. The doctors gave him a grim prognosis of a year left to live—at best. Even though I was furious at the doctors for not recognizing the lump in the earlier scans, I now know that only God decides when it's our time. It is not up to one doctor, one action, or one moment. All we can do is not take for granted the limited time we have with the ones we love on this earth. Every day we are living with broken relationships is a day we won't get back. Eventually, those days will run out.

As our family rallied around Dad and one another, we began spending more intentional time together. I made a conscious effort to visit my parents in Florida as much as I could. One day, close to the beginning of his chemo, I sat with my withered father and looked over his brittle body. His wrinkled head that used to be decorated with wisps of brown hair was now only peppered with patches of dull skin spots. Suddenly, it was all too real for me as my chest tightened like a snare and my breath became labored. Overwhelmed, I wept. Ugly, snotty tears marred my face. These sobs weren't just for my ailing father, they were also a funeral dirge mourning our unrequited relationship that would soon be coming to an earthly ending. I couldn't believe we no longer had years together, but months or maybe only weeks ... maybe days. This was the first time as an adult that my dad had ever seen me break, and I just kept crying.

But he didn't shed a tear; he just held me.

Then on January 11, 2005, almost exactly a year after he was diagnosed, my father passed away. At only sixty-seven years of age, he'd run out of time. It felt unfair, but abundance did come from my father's illness that I didn't see at the time. Although we never repaired our father-son relationship, his disease had been the cata-lyst to start the healing process and open up our lines of communication. Had my father just died in his sleep one evening without warning, I would have never had the chance to spend all that time with him during his battle with cancer.

My dad's passing was the final blow. I was already breaking down physically, and my marriage was basically over. My kids were angry with me. I was crushed, and losing my father—my mentor and role model—pushed me over the edge. I didn't know how to slow down or how to grieve, so I continued throwing myself into MOP. Work had seemingly become my crutch, and the more hours I could be occupied with business activity, the less time I was forced to deal with the painful places in my personal life. We all have those unlit spaces in our minds and souls where we try to hide away when things get too overbearing. It's a defense mechanism, and if we don't identify it, we can't change it. We will never heal and be able to fully move Up.

Besides, if I died of a heart attack while at work, at least everyone would be driven to acknowledge that I was a tireless hard worker. To be honest, in some ways, I was hoping that would happen because I so was ill-equipped to deal with my own emotions. Doubt was suddenly shrouding me as I started to wonder if life was even worth living.

When I look at our family pictures, I do so with sadness. There was a ten-year period where I never smiled. No one ever saw my teeth. It's not that I didn't know how to smile or didn't want to smile; I just felt like I had nothing to smile about. My entire being was an endless grind. In my professional life, I was fighting vehemently to get on top and stay there. In my personal life, I was stuck. Mired in a nonexistent relationship with my wife, I didn't have time to be both present for our children and present for my job. I had to choose where my time and energy were spent. I had zero balance but couldn't see it through the dense fog choking out my soul. My life was precisely what happens when you let your ego and programming rule you.

I admit my wife raised our children. I was working six days a week, and although the kids loved me, I wasn't really close to any of them. I wanted to give them the special parent-child bond that I had longed to have with my own parents growing up, but I just didn't have the time for it. At least, that's what I told myself.

During the last fifteen years of my marriage, my wife was consistently painting me in a bad light. It is true that I was not at home and that I worked too many hours, but she started a rumor that I was unfaithful. The truth is, I didn't have time or the desire to cheat. Plus, while I might be lacking in the emotional engagement department, I was not lacking in integrity. In my mind, I had envisioned walking out on my wife and our marriage, but the impact of what that would do to my children was the anchor that made me stay. Still, it felt as if I were teetering on the brink, always waiting for the straw that would break the camel's back.

One Saturday morning, it found me.

After breakfast, I was sitting at the dining room table with my coffee and newspaper. To this day, I have no idea what possessed me to read the obituaries. Before that day, I could count on one hand the number of times I'd perused that page—literally, fewer than five times. Something— call it intuition—told me to give the obits a glance, and one name instantly caught my attention. I had to read the bold type twice before my brain could catch up with what my eyes were seeing on the page. My wife's sister's father-in-law was listed in the obituaries.

I loved the old guy, and my wife knew it. We had been on numerous vacations and other outings with him throughout the years. I knew he had been sick, but I had no idea it had gotten that bad. According to the listing, he had died three days earlier, on Thursday, and here I was reading it in a newspaper instead of hearing about it from my wife. I knew she had to have been notified days earlier, which meant she intentionally hadn't told me.

I wheeled around to face my wife, and she could tell instantly by the incensed look on my face that I was furious. However, she didn't say a word and let her silence confirm my suspicions. I slammed the paper down and told her I was leaving. *Leaving the kitchen? Leaving the house? Leaving the marriage?* I didn't specify, but I'm quite certain we both knew the weight of my proclamation.

My marriage had reached the apex of dysfunction. My wife was actually a good woman, but we weren't good together. We'd both played active roles in the disintegration of our bond. I had ruined her after years of running our marriage like I ran my business, and the only way she knew to gain power in the relationship was through manipulation and withholding things from me—such as information and sex. We were a volatile cocktail as she was living her programming just like I was playing out mine.

In the middle of 2008, amidst mounting health and personal crises, I was blindsided by a lawsuit that would call my integrity and my good name into question. After my father's death, my mother's grief forced me to take care of certain elements of his estate. He was always frugal and concerned about money, so when the will was finally read it was no surprise that Dad had left Mom in good financial shape—life insurance policy, vacation home in Florida, and a car. What was surprising is that Dad had instructed my mother to sell the family house in Lexington, Ohio. Not only did this home have sentimental value because it was where my family had grown up, but also practical value as it sat directly adjacent to our family business's building. In fact, even though none of us lived there anymore, the home's yard was where we stored a portion of our work equipment.

To be honest, it felt like a strange request. I'll never know why Dad wanted us to sell my childhood home or why he didn't just want MOP to buy the property, but I intended to honor his wishes. Throwing caution to the wind, I connected my mother with a local Realtor to list the property.

Within a few weeks, we were sifting through multiple offers on the house. Ready to move quickly, I signed and accepted the one that appeared to be the best. Obviously, *best* turned out to be a relative term. In fact, *best* couldn't have been any worse.

About a week later, I was at my shop when a man approached me. I soon realized he wasn't a customer as he informed me that he had bought the house next door. I introduced myself and did my best to greet our new neighbor, but he wasn't interested in niceties.

"Tell me about what goes on down here. What kind of business are you running?" he asked. I briefly explained that MOP was a family-owned shop that did pipeline work. The truth is, he didn't care what line of work we did or how the company worked.

"We were over here around 8:00 p.m. last night and the noise from your shop was way too loud, and that's just not going to work." It was at that exact moment that I knew we had made a colossal mistake. We should have kept the property in the family.

I immediately called my attorney and told him I couldn't sell the house to the prospective buyer under contract. I knew if this deal closed, it would be heading into a perpetual battle as the new owner would be looking to shut my business down with constant complaints over what he deemed as noise pollution. I wouldn't be able to operate MOP the way it had been running for the last forty years. I assure you that no one was going to take this company, built on my recently deceased father's back, away from my family.

I wasn't sure what would happen next, but my lawyer tried to minimize my concerns by telling me that the worst thing the buyer could do was sue me for backing out. I was definitely ready to roll the dice on a potential lawsuit. At least I would still have my business and my peace of mind. Plus, how expensive could the lawsuit really be? The house was only valued at $150,000.

I called my Realtor, Carol, and told her I was no longer interested in selling the house to *anyone*. I explained how I'd met with the potential new owner who had expressed apprehension over the noise and that the conversation made me rethink the whole idea of getting rid of the house. I couldn't be beholden to anyone or anything that could hamper my business. Carol reiterated that I could be sued. I didn't care. Bring it on.

My house. My rules. End of story.

As I'd been warned, the buyer did bring a lawsuit against me for backing out of the contract. Thanks to the advice of my lawyer, I was prepared for that result. Anytime money is involved and deals go south, lawsuits are sometimes just the cost of doing business. What I wasn't prepared for was the basis of the lawsuit: racial discrimination.

This was not a simple real estate deal turned bad; this was an assassination of my character. The buyer was understandably upset, but the lawyer he'd retained insisted the reason I'd rescinded the contract was not because of my desire to keep the family business and property undisturbed, but because his client was African-American.

As someone attuned to internal anger, I recognized that this lawyer had a big chip on his shoulder, and it bled out in all his words and actions. Everything he said, as misguided as it was, went for the jugular. He bullied and belittled my first attorney so badly that she eventually resigned—leaving us scrambling to find a new legal team.

Eventually, I reached out to the potential owner and offered him $150,000 so he could buy a house, any other house he wanted. Surprisingly, he rejected my generous proposal and chose to push forward with the lawsuit. At that moment, I put a stake in the ground. If it's a fight he wanted, I decided I was going to give it to him. The attack was personal, but I don't back down to bullies. Remember Henry Simpson? I punch bullies in the face. This battle was on.

I'm now certain that God was trying to get my attention as the divorce, the lawsuit and my health—every part of my life—were collapsing spectacularly around me. The only saving grace I had was my business.

Chapter 5

BE PRESENT OR DIE

*W*hile I was doing much better about delegating tasks and continuing to hire valuable people, I was still exceedingly controlling. I demanded things be done my way. Notice the recurring theme of my life? Even though I now had the right people in place to shoulder much of my workload, I was still convinced that the only way to ensure things were executed correctly was to do them myself.

It didn't matter if MOP was riding high on success or in a cycle of struggle, I could never shake the haunting feeling that we were continually one quick misstep from going out of business. I didn't need any outside forces to exert pressure; I had first-ballot Hall-of-Famer status for my ability to put crippling pressure upon myself. I recognize now this anxiety was programmed in my childhood and was continuing to control me as an adult.

Here I was holding myself down again. It's so easy to do this with destructive self-talk, and oftentimes the loudest voice we hear is our own. This internal dialogue can influence everything from our self-esteem to our physical health. We as humans have an insane ability to manifest what we speak to ourselves. Call it a self-fulfilling prophecy, but if you are constantly beating yourself up, you will always be a victim. I wasn't at a point to understand that yet in my journey, but *how* we talk and think of ourselves matters. Be aware. For most of us, negative self-talk has become so routine that we don't even recognize it anymore. It's time to see it for what it is and silence it!

In my line of work, the dangers are real and the stakes are high. I would often hear about a company losing an employee on a jobsite accident that could have been easily avoided with a little precaution. Even at my own sites, I'd see workers distracted by cell phones and other minor annoyances. It is a normal human trait—the mind wants to be everywhere else but in the present. Nevertheless, my team was not as focused as they should have been, and I had to take our safety measures to higher levels. In our industry, no one can afford for employees' minds to be anywhere other than on their present tasks at hand. They had to forget about yesterday and not dream about tomorrow. The more I dipped into this realization at MOP, the more I explored what it meant to be truly *present*.

I decided to put my energy into changing our culture of focus. I made it a point to speak about it often and connect with my workers in a way that made them understand the importance of attention. I discovered focus was something you turned off and on and could be learned if it didn't come naturally. Like most things, focus can be cultivated through intentional practice.

"I need your mind not just while you are on the jobsite, but before you get to the jobsite. This is not just a 9-to-5 job. If you are awake, I need you." It was a bold statement, but a necessary one if my employees were to grasp the magnitude of what I was demanding.

At that time, it was the only way I knew to explain my desire for my employees to be present. Of course, some were more receptive than others. However, my intention was to affect the philosophy of our company, and that typically takes brash statements and unflinching moves.

After months of *my* focus on *their* focus, the results were obvious. Whether by practice or osmosis, MOP employees became more present at work, which in turn generated more efficiency as a team. With our newfound concentration, business kept increasing and I was flowing like a rock star at work. I was very intentional when communicating with my employees. There is an old adage that I recalled from my college athletic days—nobody wants to win for a coach they don't like. It's absolutely true in sports, and it's accurate in business as well. If you want your team to run through a wall for you, you rally around them and make all the players better, just like ol' MJ and his '96 Chicago Bulls. When you trust your players and make them feel valued, everybody wins. That is true leadership.

While business was inspiring, back at home I was wedged deep in the middle of a nasty divorce proceeding. The propaganda against me was in full force. Every small misstep and lazy, cross word was neatly typed up in a deposition to be preserved in the annals of the courts. I knew my worst fear would be realized, and my kids would be dragged into this demoralizing process.

At that point, I still didn't know how to properly present my emotions. Even where I am now, I realize the communication lesson is going to be a lifelong learning process. Instead of dealing with my martial situation and the potential fallout with my children, I went right back to the one place where I knew I could find some comfort: work. Allowing my job to monopolize all my time and energy, I concocted new business moves that

I subconsciously hoped would fill the voids left in my mind, body, and spirit by my personal life.

With all the drama, I felt that diversifying my assets would be a prudent plan. As our natural gas company had worked with so many construction firms over the decades, I was completely comfortable with building contractors and knew the ins and outs of their trade. It only made sense that real estate would be a logical complement to my natural gas company. Plus, home construction wasn't completely foreign to me, as I had previously built several condos. I'd had enough development experience to understand the metrics of the business model, so I started looking for opportunities.

Reflecting back, my "push forward at all costs" mentality was glaringly obvious. If I slowed down, there was the possibility that all my personal baggage would catch up to me. As long as I was accelerating forward at breakneck speeds, I wouldn't have to deal with my personal demons. I was constantly moving forward, but never moving Up. There is a difference.

Candidly, I was the one who needed the diversification, not my assets. Instead of adding more to my plate and grinding harder at work, it would have been an ideal time to deal with my personal shortcomings. A moment of pause could have allowed me the chance to get grounded and more centered, but I didn't know any of that back then. I lacked any depth as a one-sided, one-dimensional being sleepwalking through life. Sadly, that lone dimension wasn't family, faith, or fun. It was work.

The popular investment strategy at that time was to purchase an apartment complex and convert it into condos. With an apartment complex, the income stream comes from monthly rental fees, but condos are sold individually and you can recoup your investment faster. At first, I considered jumping into the prevailing conversion approach like the other money guys were doing, but that just wouldn't be me, would it? Never one to walk the beaten path that others were traveling, I went bigger and badder. I decided to heighten the risk-reward ratio and build my condo complex from the ground up. Plan settled.

My research guided me to a prominent trend of potential buyers wanting to purchase homes within sixty to one hundred miles from the Gulf of Mexico. As I scoured cities and crunched numbers, I discovered that Dothan, Alabama, fit all the metrics. All the necessary boxes were checked off, including average income, population growth, and average age of the residents, yet there were currently no condos within the city limits. Immediately I leapt at the opportunity to shine where others shied away. It was time to break some ground.

With blueprints for 120 units and a clubhouse, this would be no small undertaking. It was incumbent on my team and me to build the entire infrastructure from scratch. This meant that roads, electrical, and sewers needed to be planned and constructed before we could even start any work on the actual condos. My financial situation was leaner than ever, and any of the remaining money or credit I was able to salvage from the divorce went into this ambitious project. Splitting time between

Alabama and Ohio to make everything work, I had asked for and now certainly received a distraction from my personal life.

For better or worse.

About that same time, I approached my son, Jordan, about possibly working with me. Twenty-two and a recent graduate with a double major in finance and entrepreneurship from Miami University in Ohio, he was eager to make his mark on the world. I appreciated his fervent desire and knew I wanted him somewhere on my team, but ultimately it was up to him. I didn't want to press anything upon him as my father had done before with me. Besides, I was confident Jordan would have the chance to develop quicker if he were calling his own shots.

I didn't want to hire Jordan only because he was my son. I had complete confidence in him. Whether it was a conscious decision or not, MOP or a condo project would serve the same purpose as the family shop did for my father and me during my childhood. I was hopeful that my son and I could create a deeper connection with each other through business, even if I wasn't sure how to comprehensively approach it. For me, it would prove to be a tightrope walk of balancing mentorship while trying not to repeat the mistakes of my past. Working together was going to lead to one of two polemic options—we'd either grow closer or the pressure would drive us further apart. It was a risky alignment, as family and work always seem to be, but it was a necessary leap of faith.

An effortless intellectual with a passionate work ethic, Jordan was someone who I really did want to see come under the MOP umbrella. I also recognized that, although he'd been around the business his whole life, he didn't understand it at a granular level. Growing up, he had always been adjacent to the family business and didn't have a childhood similar to mine where I learned everything on-site with the construction workers. Jordan was going to have to go into the field to get a deeper understanding of the business if he wanted to excel. I needed him to understand how to physically operate inside the grittiest parts of the job so that he would be able to translate that information from the field to the office. Once he had a grasp on the ground-floor workflow, I knew he would be best suited to move into a fiscal position figuring out overhead, margins, and rates to charge our customers. Bidding is an art where you must understand how to do the work before you understand how to bid it.

However, Jordan had recently gotten married and his wife wasn't keen on him being on the road. The role at MOP would require a fair amount of travel, spending days on sites overseeing the work progress and managing the crews. That's a hard life for a newlywed couple, and it was a sage decision by his wife.

I decided the best solution was for Jordan to be a site manager for the Alabama condo project instead of bringing him into the pipeline company. He would get some firsthand experience dealing with banks and construction crews while being my full-time eyes, ears, and voice when I was elsewhere. It was the perfect bedrock situation for my son to build the confidence and experience he would need for larger roles later in his career.

I thought pursuing more business ventures would give me peace, but it really gave me more stress. Soon after the Alabama project was rolling, I fell ill again. This wasn't uneasy stomach pain you push through; this was much worse.

Staying at Jordan's house in Dothan, I woke up around midnight to go to the bathroom. No sooner had I opened the door and flipped on the light than everything went pitch-black. I don't really remember passing out, but I do remember falling backward from a standing position and slamming my head against the cold floor tiles. I was told there were likely some convulsions somewhere in the mix too.

At the hospital, the doctors couldn't figure out what was wrong with me, as all of my test results came back negative. This was good news for me, but it confused the medical staff. Confounding things even more, there were still no concrete answers with the follow-up appointments. Unsure of a diagnosis, the doctors were advising me not to drive because they were worried I could have another onset of seizures or convulsions at any time.

I managed to keep my driver's license, but within a few months of that incident, things went further south after I contracted a potentially deadly MRSA infection. My face and ears were both visibly and embarrassingly affected. Soon after, my feet and ankles started giving me major problems. Out of the blue, I found myself suddenly needing a cane and then crutches to walk. There was zero doubt that I was breaking down mentally and physically. When one aching foot would start to feel better, the other would become increasingly problematic. Diabetes and gout had been ruled out. With no prior injuries to my feet, the perplexed doctors struggled to explain my rapidly deteriorating condition.

It didn't make any sense to me then, but it certainly does now. The burden of overwhelming stress and emotions has to live somewhere. My body was holding on to all of it and had finally reached its limit. After decades, the aggregate stress and trauma had exceeded the threshold of my mind and soul to manifest physically. My negative patterns—*never back down, win at all costs, grind harder, success at all costs*—were literally killing me.

I wasn't living. I was dying. Things couldn't get worse.

Then the financial crisis of 2008 hit like a hammer. Actually, it was more like an atom bomb. Midyear, we had all the infrastructure of the condos built with eight beautiful buildings and the clubhouse standing. At this stage, my investors and I had already sunk a couple of million dollars into the project, and we would soon need more to continue the buildout. Due to the imploding financial environment, the bank carrying our loans was getting pressure from government regulators to clamp down. In turn, they started hassling us, and I knew it was only a matter of time before they pulled out of our project completely.

Over the next couple of months, my bank kept tabs on our progress and tracked every movement because it was worried I'd default on the loan. If that wasn't bad enough, back in Ohio, my business and personal banker also started questioning its financial risk inside our partnerships. Before I knew it, it had pulled out of MOP's business; a banking relationship that I'd had for twenty years was suddenly gone. I'd lost my community, my wife, my family, my good name, a great deal of money in that legal battle, and now my bank had dumped me. Talk about being at an all-time low.

Nine months later, the financial crisis was at its peak and wreaking havoc on everyone. By then, Jordan and I had built the new condo development, but our bank in Alabama was done with me too. This was no surprise as it had finally deemed our project carried too much risk for it.

That made my situation extremely tricky as I had to expediently find another money source or we would default and the bank would put a lien on my project. With a lien, I would be unable to legally sell the property. That would trigger the bank to take the next step and foreclose. All that my son and I had worked for, risked, and built would be lost.

I was certain it was goodnight, Alabama.

I didn't have the money to cover our note, and I had already bet big by putting all my cash into developing the properties. The Alabama condo project alone included sixteen homes, a clubhouse, and the infrastructure for 120 units. That need to have a distraction in my life was coming at a very heavy cost. Moreover, it would shatter me even further to let my son down. The prospect of Jordan seeing me as a failure motivated me more than the potential loss of the debilitating amounts of cash. Furthermore, I had two additional friends who had trusted me and invested heavily in the condo project— just more people to let down.

I was beyond desperate and barely above groveling. As I exhausted my options, I found one outside chance to get the money and keep our real estate dream from collapsing. I located a legitimate private lender who was willing to loan me the necessary money . . . for 35 percent interest! The rate was horrific, worse than any credit card rate I had ever seen, but still within the legal limits. It was a do-or-die situation where the project would have to endure the insane interest rate or lose everything to the bank.

Unfortunately, the extortionate fees didn't stop there. On the day I went to sign the loan papers, this new lender must have smelled blood in the water. He knew my predicament and decided to take further advantage of it by telling me that upon paying off the loan, he would require an additional $50,000. He wanted me to consider it a *closing fee*.

That lender didn't get a signature from me that day, but he did receive a colorful selection of choice words. I'm pretty sure I punched out his teeth ... in my mind. In reality, I went back to the office with my tail between my legs to let Jordan know the devastating news. I've never felt so inadequate as a father or an entrepreneur.

The physical weight of my stress continued to debilitate my body. My weakened mind had shut down and my energy was at an all-time low. In the midst of my collapsing health, my divorce was finalized. My ex-wife got half, which consisted primarily of our house, cash, and investments. My half was all I wanted: the company. I had MOP, a failing condo project, and the financial calamity of 2008 swallowing me whole.

I went down to the Gulf Shores to clear my head. More accurately, I went there to avoid people and conversation. I was angry. Disappointed. Frustrated. Broken. Life hadn't turned out the way I'd planned.

I didn't have a single person who I truly felt comfortable asking for help, but that was my own doing. I had shut everyone out. I had wanted to do this life all by myself and had been too proud to ask for help. These compounded stressors created an "emotional arthritis" that made my body and brain hurt at all times. Even if I had a minor success, I couldn't enjoy it because I was convinced that something else would happen to immediately steal even that little happiness away from me. The pain was too great.

I wanted *out*.

Walking along the beach, I began to feel a magnetic pull from the rolling whitecaps forty yards out. I staggered to where the water rushed over the sand in waves, and I froze. Watching wave after wave roll in, I stared out at the blue abyss until the wet sand began to collapse under my weight. The siren's call beckoned me to keep walking out into the depths of the angry ocean. I could disappear and no one would notice. Or even if someone eventually did, it would be too late. In those moments of quiet contemplation, I thought about my kids, my business, and what little I had left of my faith. I was a complete failure in each part of my life. Maybe everyone and everything would be better if I weren't around.

I closed my eyes and took another step into the waves. Then, another. As I descending into the swirling void, I felt an overwhelming sense of peace. It was as if the wrathful waves and tossing water were perfectly mirroring my inner turmoil. Even though I was getting pounded by the surf, the stress in my body suddenly clicked off like a light switch. I was prepared to keep pushing forward to a place from which I might not return.

I stood in the water with my eyes closed and my brain mentally checked out. Surrendering to my circumstances, I continued forward step by step. As the water surrounded me, I had no sense of time. Time is completely irrelevant when you're ending your life. Submerged, I persisted forward and felt the water splash above my shoulders as my feet struggled to make contact with the ocean floor. As my head finally made it under the water, I just knew I would find the peace I was so desperately seeking.

Instead, something very different happened. Suddenly, I was scared as hell. My eyes exploded open with a shot of adrenaline as I coughed up salty water. My body was letting me know that I was lying to myself! I didn't want to die. In actuality, I was terrified of death because I still had so much life left to live, even though my foggy mind could not see it. I turned my back on the raging waves and slogged my way to dry land. When I got to the beach, I lay in the sand and stared up at the endless stars punching through the night sky. For a moment, the world felt very big and my problems very small!. I realized that what I really wanted was to be a better man, father, and leader.

That incident proved to me that if I didn't make a change, I would die in Lexington, Ohio. I've always envisioned my hometown shrouded in darkness and gloom, an agonizing reminder of everything that had gone wrong in my life, buoyed by the distressing ghosts of failed relationships—all my mistakes and bad choices laid bare for the people around me to judge and place blame. Even the lawsuit for racial discrimination was an albatross around my neck, drowning my name in the public sphere of gossip. There was no way I could survive, much less thrive, in that environment.

While I didn't yet understand the concept of healing and going Up, I knew I had to shed the shame and guilt that was pinning me down. I needed to become a brand-new person. Not only did I need a change of scenery, pace, and energy, I needed to find a place that could lead me to reset everything. In order to give myself a fighting chance, I made the proactive choice to go where I could feel free.

At that point, I was forty-eight years old and wasn't convinced that I would live to see fifty.

Chapter 6

WAKING UP IN
THE DESERT

*P*hoenix, Arizona.

I had visited Phoenix once in 2006 to catch my beloved Ohio State Buckeyes put a whuppin' on Notre Dame's Fighting Irish at the thirty-fifth annual Fiesta Bowl. I remember connecting with the vitality and vibe of the people in Arizona in a way that was different from anything I had experienced in Ohio. Sitting there in Sun Devil Stadium, I recall thinking at the time that when my youngest child left home, and if my marriage didn't work out, I could move to Arizona. Finally, I found myself brave enough to put that premonition to the test.

Winter always brought a quantifiable lull in our MOP business, and compounded with the ongoing crisis of 2008, this season looked not only to be slow, but, a complete standstill. With that knowledge I approached our leadership team to talk to them about me wintering in Phoenix and running our business from there. My team must have suspected that I needed a change; they were very supportive of my decision with the caveat that I would still need to travel back every two weeks to keep a presence in Ohio. So in October 2008 I started commuting between Phoenix and Ohio with the thought of it just being for the winter.

In my mind, there was no temporariness to it. Arizona was not a layover, but, a destination in my journey. The air was clean. The mountains were incredible. The residents were kind. There was such a persuasive pull that coincided with the idea of healing and escaping. I couldn't put my finger on it then, and in many ways I still can't, but there is a restorative, curative property about Arizona.

I took almost nothing to Phoenix. I literally had a single suitcase and the clothes I wore on the plane. I needed as few things in my life that tied me to Ohio as possible. If I were going to start fresh, I had to leave everything behind—material items included.

With no place to live, I called my cousin Greg Herbert. I didn't want to impose (though it was), but I hoped I could crash with his family while I looked for a place to rent. I'm not sure if he will ever know how much his *yes* meant to me. His family gave me support, love, and a place to regroup during a very uncertain time in my life. I couldn't have made the transition without them, and his family became my safe haven. Locating a select few honest people who have your best interest at heart is a vital foundation for any kind of personal development and healing.

I had to change quite a few things about my life, but I didn't know what that was going to look like, or how I was going to make it happen. One thing I did know was that change is painful. If I wanted my future years to be different from my first forty-seven, I had to be committed and intentional about moving Up and not remain stuck in my past. Even though I wasn't sure where I would end up at the end of my journey, it took the slight motion of that first step to send me on my way.

This was my awakening.

With this move to Arizona, I began slowly gaining momentum. I couldn't help but notice that, although my determination had fueled my success and carried me far in life, there must be something more vital that fills in the gaps. My me-against-the-world attitude had forced me to do this life on my own, and it was destroying me. I was determined to find that bigger force that could carry me and lead me forward when all I wanted to do was crumble. This life required more strength than I humanly possessed. Looking back, just like the ubiquitous poem "Footprints," He was always there. I just needed to slow down and find Him.

Faith is a multifaceted journey. By its enigmatic nature, it can be counterintuitive and difficult to grasp. When you are at your lowest, it can take heroic proportions of faith to believe that your life has value on this earth. When things are going really well, it's easy to forget about God altogether. More than anything, faith is trust. Above all, that trust is about relying on something greater than you.

Let me preface this by saying that I think I knew *of* God, but I didn't *know* God. I was brought up in the Church of Christ and baptized when I was eight. Throughout my youth and adult years, I was a Sunday churchgoer, but I wouldn't say I was a beacon for others. I doubt anyone could have walked into my office on a random Tuesday and said, "This man is a follower of Christ."

Think of that guy at the Christmas party who is the best storyteller, cutting it up with his first-rate jokes. You'll always find him surrounded by a throng of eggnog-guzzling people—laughing and regaling with every hilarious word he speaks. You know who this guy is, and you've seen him at all the functions, but you've never really been intentional about meeting him. You're content to just stand on the edges and chuckle at appropriate times so you fit in. That was where my faith was; I knew enough to recognize God but was more comfortable never getting into the circle. It was better to just watch Him work from afar. However, I soon discovered that inside the circle is where the genuine power lies. The healing only happens when you truly get to know that gregarious guy holding court in the middle of the circle. So you build a relationship with him. He no longer becomes someone you bump into at parties, but he's somebody you communicate with on a daily basis.

Matt, an old friend who lived in Columbus, knew I was spending time in Phoenix to try to find much-needed peace and healing. He also recognized that I was out there alone and took it upon himself to tell a local pastor, Russell Johnson, about me. Russell obviously didn't know me, but just because of his nature he cared about me. Without ever having spoken so much as a word to me, Pastor Johnson sent me *The Maxwell Leadership Bible* with the most thoughtful note enclosed:

> May the God of Amazing Grace give you great joy for the journey. He has enabled you to be the Prince of Privilege. I pray that this sacred trust will be a blessing to many. Only in heaven will you realize the full reach of your God-given potential. May His peace and His wisdom guide your steps. May the love and mercy of God strengthen your days.
>
> Your brother in His service,
> Russell

I began reading bits of the Bible over the next few weeks and was astounded by the blatantly direct connection between business leadership and my faith. *The Maxwell Leadership Bible* redefined my concept of leadership by placing it inside sound biblical context. I had always been an honest businessman with a company that was rooted in providing a good service at a fair price. As far as I was concerned, that was the totality of what was required of me to be an ethical leader. However, Maxwell's notes pointed me to the places in the Bible that helped me understand my leadership was not limited to overseeing job specifications and time-tables. I also had a responsibility to be an example to those who worked with me so they could get closer to God. I'd never considered that before, but as my mind opened, so did my eyes. Suddenly I could see the opportunities to practice this radical leadership in real life materialize in front of me.

We've established that throughout my life when I do anything, I go big. So it should come as no surprise that I found myself at the largest church in Phoenix. Let me be clear on this one—I didn't find the church, the church found me! My buddy Matt's unprompted mention about me to Russell led to an unsolicited call from Russell to a elder by the name of Mac McElroy, who reached out and invited me to Christ Church of the Valley. It was evident that God was working through His people to get me connected to Him on a higher level.

At that time, Christ Church of the Valley had services for around fifteen thousand people every Sunday and was the fastest-growing congregation in America.

(Today, CCV averages thirty-two thousand attendees for Sunday services.) Hearing a sermon in that fifteen-thousand-seat expanse can feel more like an arena experience than something that goes down at a sanctuary. Not many people have experienced a church this large, and it can be easy to feel like a nobody when you're out in the immense wave of anonymous people filling the pews. Quite frankly, for once I found myself enjoying the anonymity.

The reality is that I appreciated the obscurity because I couldn't imagine having anything of value to contribute to a congregation this massive. However, as I was focusing on my overall growth, I knew I had to take the plunge. Even if it was uncomfortable, I was desperate to go deeper and find something spiritually different than the tepid faith of my past. My new life journey was holistic, and nothing was paramount to finding that spiritual connection and dynamism.

The perfect opening for me to get involved with the church at the top level emerged when Mac, who had been treating me like a son, introduced me to Dr. Don Wilson, the senior pastor and founder of CCV. I knew his messages were resonating with me every Sunday, but to connect with him on personal level over dinner was a welcome surprise. Sometimes we can put pastors on such a high pedestal that we forget they are just like us, trying to navigate life while dealing with their own issues. Don was a gem and just the type of person I needed in my life to shift my spiritual side into a higher gear.

I had been involved in my home church back in Lexington and had even helped to build a church about eight years before my divorce. As we got to know each other, Don learned about my profession, my company, and my community presence in Ohio. The timing was right, and I proudly informed Don I was ready to be of use at the church. *Surely*, I thought, *he might ask me to lead a new construction project or something else of great significance.*

"You can start on the sidewalk."

My gasp was, unfortunately, audible. I was quick to reply, "Like a greeter? On the sidewalk?"

Don nodded.

Well, that was not *exactly* what I'd had in mind. In fact, his suggestion entered polar-opposite territory. I owned a multimillion-dollar business. As an overachiever who had played semi-pro golf and college basketball, everything I did was competitive as I strived to be the best. My guess was that the best weren't enlisted to greet some faceless pedestrians with a wave or smile out on the sidewalk at one of fifteen entrances to the church.

Needless to say, my ego was instantly triggered by a prideful Spidey-sense. I wanted to do something fun but at a high-level of leadership with the church. Esteemed. Vaunted. I was used to being up front, not out front. I could tell this was Don's final offer and there would be no budging. So I choked down my pride and surrendered my vision of grandeur.

I'm so glad I did because Pastor Wilson proved to be right.

Around this same time I felt ready to move out of Greg's house. He wasn't pressuring me to leave, but I was ready to have a place to myself and allow his household to get back to normal.

On any journey, you're constantly looking for signs of confirmation that the path you're traveling is the right one. When I pulled up to the Omni Scottsdale Resort & Spa at Montelucia for the first time and laid eyes on Camelback Mountain, I felt like this was one of those special moments. The signs couldn't have been clearer than if they had been in giant neon letters accompanied by fireworks and a marching band.

Not only is the mountain captivating with the magnificent pinkish red boulder that forms its namesake shape, but the resort itself has a certain magical affinity about it. With lush greenery, vibrant flowers, and palm trees whose fronds dance in the breeze, the entrance to Montelucia is as inviting as it is enchanting. I had little doubt this would be my new home for healing.

Physical activity was still brutal for me, but the brilliance of Camelback Mountain beckoned me daily. I longed to one day walk that rugged landscape, but even that idea felt nearly impossible. I was still struggling to make it up stairs without my crutches. A few steps would leave me gasping for air. However, I knew if I ever wanted to achieve my goal of hiking Camelback, I had to be more active—even if that meant starting small.

I knew I wasn't ready to tackle the mountain, but if I pushed myself, I could make the rounds of Montelucia. The resort has an amazing outdoor reception area with its front desk under an open-air structure held up by large columns. In its center, a large water feature greets you with the soothing rhythm of flowing water. As you move through to the inner courtyard, additional water features lead to the pool area, the grandeur of Camelback rising behind like a painted backdrop. As I began my daily walks, I could always spy my mountain summoning me in the background.

I contemplated many things during those walks.

Two thousand miles away from Ohio and the stress of work, it was a blessing to breathe the pure the air and have time to decompress and reflect. Each day as I would walk a little farther, a little longer, I would long for more. I had a mountain in front of me that had to be tackled, and I knew the only way to get myself back into some physical version of readiness was to find a gym. With that summit goal in mind, I put my limitations to the side and started training.

Well...training might be an overstatement.

I fumbled around with the treadmills and weight equipment—a constant reminder that I hadn't been working out or taking care of my body back in Ohio. As soon as my physical body had begun to fail, I no longer valued it. As an athlete, if I couldn't get into a weight room and throw 325 on a bench press like the good ol' days, I didn't want to be a part of it. My ego simply wouldn't allow it. But my intentionality and mindset shift pushed that Old Brent ego aside and assigned me a new, simple objective: just get my body moving. It hurt like hell most days, and I prepared myself that my progress was not going to be made in heroic leaps and bounds. I would have to walk this path with clumsy infant steps, but I had to keep advancing to go Up.

One morning at the gym, as I was staring out the window at that magical mountain and dreaming about the day when I could finally scale it, I felt an arm slide around my shoulder.

"How ya doing?"

I turned to see a complete stranger with a gracious smile on his face. He introduced himself as Tom and told me he was a personal trainer. Even though he didn't know me from Adam, there was something about how authentically he spoke that made me believe his question was a genuine one.

His disposition was so inviting and calming that I found myself open to explaining my health issues. My limitations didn't seem to shake Tom at all as he never lost his smile. With total confidence, he said he was absolutely certain he could lead me to regain my physical strength. His certainty was contagious and his expertise was convincing. Somehow, I already trusted him. Besides, I had nothing to lose and everything to gain at that point.

I became Tom's personal project as he poured positivity into my life like no one had ever done—no man, no woman, not even my father. It is absolutely remarkable what being around encouraging people can do for your health. With Tom, I discovered there is a truth to speaking life and letting go of the negativity that sinks us. Tom had a connection to the world I had never experienced before. This guy was tuned in and present in just about everything with ease and serenity. I was inspired, not just to work out harder, but to find that same peace and holistic approach to life. I started eating better. I started sleeping better. I started looking better. For the first time in a long time, I saw evidence that my life was starting to improve. With Tom's help, I began to put together the pieces of a puzzle that I didn't know had existed regarding my health and overall wellness.

My physical training was driven by a functional approach using resistance, in the form of weights, straps, and bands, against the body's natural movements. Instead of binding up the muscles from the unnatural angles of machines and heavy lifting, we would lengthen and strengthen the muscles, all while supporting my joints, ligaments, and tendons. Tom's regimen was laser-focused on core strength, stability, stretching, and functional training. It was a foreign perspective on fitness for me, but as I committed to it I saw evidence that it worked. Since I'd been a college athlete, I knew what hard work looked and felt like, but functional training was a brand-new world.

Ultimately, I started to realize that in order to be centered in my life, I had to learn what it meant to be centered physically. I had to learn to eat from a place of honoring myself from the inside out. It was a novel idea for me that food was not just for pleasure, but was also the fuel that powered my body. It's simple, really. If you fill a Corvette engine with low-budget, low-octane gas, the car will never have the chance to operate at its full capacity. In the same way, food is meant to be functional.

With positive moves Up, Tom focused on eliminating the junk from my life that was detrimental to my health. It was amazing to learn so much more about what my body was supposed to do and how I was meant to train it from the inside out—both with food and strength.

When I did things that were damaging to my body, I was making willful statements that my body wasn't valuable. These toxic actions might seem small and insignificant, but they are actually symptoms of a much larger self-worth issue. I began observing how my eating and drinking habits affected my personality and body.

I began paying attention to what I ate. If something upset my stomach, I had to realize it was because my body didn't want it. It makes perfect sense now, but I had never connected the dots of why my stomach would become upset. I only thought to grab some antacid to help it out and didn't give it a second thought. I realized that if I were eating effectively, my body needed to play a more pivotal role in my food selection than my mind did. Suddenly I was aware that my body was signaling to me at all times. When I chose to listen, I was amazed at how much my body really talked to me and let me know what honored it.

I learned that all of these actions and choices cumulatively fed my core, my foundation. Without physicality, it's hard to gain forward momentum or to be ambitious in any other way. I wanted to be hasty and to get on that mountain as soon as possible. However, it was imperative to be patient to allow my body and mind the suitable time to heal through proper nourishment and functional strength training. I didn't need giant pecs and enviable quads; what I needed were basic stability and balance. I longed to be able to pick something up off the ground or bend over without pain or imbalance. As I got stronger, lifting weights, isometrics, and hill climbing were all parts of my exercise regimen.

Finally the day came when I was ready to try Camelback with Tom. It was one of those magical mornings with crisp air and the sunrise painting those beautiful mountain trails a radiant golden hue. I stood at the base without my crutches and looked up at my task. I took that first step.

That day was a success—one that would be measured in increments. I didn't make it all the way to the top, but I was going Up! Each day I would return and go a little farther. Eventually, I was able to run Camelback Mountain with Tom. Thinking about it now still brings a smile to my face because it signaled the initial part of my arrival at better health. For the first time I had used positive fuel to motivate myself, and it had paid off it an unbelievable way. I kept pushing myself and after six months of work, I could take folks twenty years younger than me for runs around the switchbacks and smoke every one of them. Camelback quickly became my happy place where I felt accomplished, free, and clear-minded.

This truly was the first time in my entire life that I had committed to self-care, and it became the second pillar of the New Brent after my spiritual restructuring. Not only is treating your body like a temple biblical, but it is a key part to living a full and abundant experience here on earth. When that awareness sets in, it automatically starts changing your subconscious value and worth.

As soon as I began shifting my mind away from work and seeking balance, influential people seemed to enter my life whether I was ready for them or not. I met Al Fuentes by chance at an Arizona Cardinals football game and his business card read, "Mental Champ, Performance Coaching Services." I wasn't exactly sure what a performance coach was or why I would ever need one, but I flipped the card over and continued to read: "Learn the secrets to energizing the body while calming the mind to create peak performance. Ultimate Focus. In the Zone. Extraordinary Results."

Hmm . . .

That is exactly what I was interested in doing. Tom had been fixing my physical body, and spiritually I was growing daily. Al seemed like he could be just the right person to keep my healthy momentum moving Up by engaging my mind. I took the card and told him I *might* call.

Meeting with Al would be a bold move and the toughest breakthrough in my transition from unhealthy to healthy. I had never talked with anyone before about my private thoughts and overall mindset. I certainly hadn't had an open or successful counseling experience with my wife the one time we gave it a shot. I was still programmed that emotions were to be locked away deep in my psyche, never to be revealed. My whole life had been a process of concentrating on my work so that I never had to focus on my feelings. Nervous to being raw and exposed, I wasn't ready to move fully into some sort of session with Al, so I asked him if we could just grab a meal together. I simply needed an initial conversation light enough to get a better understanding of this man and his process.

During that lunch, I learned that Al is a man of faith, and we share the same athlete's mentality for victory.

Having been an All-American wrestler and national qual-ifier in the pole vault in college means he understands the intensity required to accomplish grand things.

Our connection wasn't merely about our glory days on the field (Al had been on a journey very similar to my own). Restless and unfulfilled by his accomplish-ments in college, he began to feel his worldly definition of success was coming up short. After extended bouts of unhappiness, Al realized he was mentally unprepared to succeed in life and more inclined to self-sabotage than perform. For the next seventeen years, he went on a deep-diving soul trek as he longed to understand why he and others weren't emotionally and mentally equipped for bigger and better things. That expedition brought him to a new understanding of what it means to have an *accomplished* life. He was speaking my language, and I was eager to tap in, even if it meant tough bouts of hand-holding to pull me Up.

At first, I didn't know what to expect from Al's process, and that was undoubtedly a good thing. The first few sessions were extremely sensitive. In fact, I ventured into untapped places in my heart and mind that brought out anguish, tears . . . and eventually release. If there's one thing I've learned, it's that having someone willing to be an empathetic ear to listen your ideas, emotions, and thoughts is a key part of life growth.

When you solely consider your own perspective and opinions, you pile more and more junk on top of all the negative rubbish already stored in your head. Remember: your words and thoughts have the ability to inspire and elevate you or to hold you down. Without help, you may never be able to dig yourself out of the heap. It can easily slide into a one-dimensional thought process—an echo chamber that can only amplify your biggest fears, worries, and insecurities. Giving an audible voice to your thoughts allows you to get things off your chest, and a trusted outsider's perspective can be a truly comforting relief. With that said, it's important to work with a professional who can handle and aid those conversations in order to really be able to break through. This profound type of soul-searching is different from the occasional venting to friends.

I learned that my mindset was stunting and binding me to a particular way of evaluating life. I was starting the path to getting better, but I still had the fight and grind storming inside of me. Now, that fighter mentality was subconsciously pushing back against Al's work as part of my internal self-sabotage. I was my own worst enemy, and this process was revealing how much my stubborn programming really was the author of my story.

When we first started working together, Al gave me simple homework to do, such as journaling my thoughts. I didn't think much of it at the time, but after those first few sessions, it became clear how fast my mind was spinning at all times. I was unable to shut down the speed or volume of how much *stuff* I constantly had banging through my brain. I became alert to how my mind was totally out of control. I needed to get to a place where I was the one controlling my thoughts, instead of my thoughts controlling me.

It is so easy to get caught up in everyday busyness and not create an awareness of your thoughts. We are constantly trying to load our jam-packed lives to capacity. Until you are intentional, you won't realize that you're running at a speed that will burn you out. Slowing down with my journal and thoughts was crucial. Writing without judgment is another necessary element. You'll want zero barriers or reasons to slow your process. If you can begin to create alertness around your mind and feelings, you are taking the first steps in the right direction.

Once I became cognizant of my thoughts, I could match them to the programming behind them. Identifying the issue, I was able to evaluate each life experience and its result. We've been programmed our entire lives to behave and believe the way we do. Most of it comes from our childhood experiences, but we are constantly conforming and responding to stimuli that are outside our best interests. Just like any other muscle, the brain needs to be flexed and exercised to get stronger. The only way to change old patterns is to reprogram your brain and fix the faulty issues.

Al taught me how to use visualization and meditation to calm my inner storm by providing a safe place to release my frustrations without feeling judged or jaded. I still carried a great deal of resentment and guilt from the mistakes in my life. By taking some authority and responsibility for my past, I was able to let the old programming go little by little. As the Old Brent softened, I was more open to kindness, compassion, and acceptance.

Al's approach to visualization combines breathing techniques that connect the body and activate the back of the brain. This exercise puts your mind into a state of recovery, much like when you sleep. As you start to generate theta brainwaves, your brain produces energy to retrain the subconscious mind. Done correctly, this is much more than visualizing an image or an outcome. This is a truly rigorous mental workout.

As an athlete, thinking of the brain like a trainable muscle really resonated with me, and I knew how to put in the necessary work to get the desired results. It didn't mean that the exercises were painless or undemanding; I assure you they weren't. With countless external and internal influences keeping you buried in your old, restrictive mindset, it takes sincere discipline and consistency to rewrite the brain. You can have the will to change, but if you do not put in the dedicated practice, I assure you it won't work. However, just as the wrong mindset will keep you stuck and pull you away from your potential, the right mindset will give you that boost of insight and confidence that allows you to operate at a higher level. Stay focused on your target, put in the work, and you will go Up faster than you ever expected.

Chapter 7

A SUPERHERO
OF SOUL

*S*undays had quickly become my favorite day of the week. After a month of pre-service greetings on the sidewalk, I was really starting to enjoy this time. Overall, I was in a place where I was feeling better about myself as a whole and meeting a lot of new people at CCV. My Sundays were now full of countless conversations, high fives, and smiles that meant my week started with positive energy.

I was in a miraculous place with my healing. Physically, I couldn't believe that only a year prior I had been sick and using crutches, with doctors assuring me that I needed to give up my driver's license. Mentally, my ego would have never allowed me to be in the "lowly" position of church greeter. When my mind was so work-focused, I found it so much simpler to donate my money instead of my time due to my schedule. With renewed enthusiasm and gratitude for life, I now stood confidently on the sidewalk and greeted thousands of people on their way to worship their Creator.

However, even as I was ascending, my latent ego still crept around in my body. I started hearing the same refrain from many of the families who I was greeting on their way inside:

"Have you seen Chris? Where's Chris? Is Chris around?"

Over and over, I heard these questions swirl in the ether as people walked past my greeting station. Extending beyond personal conversations, it finally got to the point where congregants began walking up and asking me straight out if I knew where to find this *magical* Chris. The truth is, I had no idea who the guy was, but I could only assume he was part of the pastoral staff or in a leadership position. Certainly, he wasn't another greeter...dare I say...competition?

Who is Chris, and what's this guy got going on that I don't?

The next Sunday came along and I was dressed to the nines in my elevated attire per usual. Fueled on coffee and joy, my energy level was high as I worked the droves of people making their ways in from the parking lot. As these folks passed by me, they received a generous smile and a "Have a blessed service!"

Then I started to hear it: "Where is Chris? Have you seen Chris today?"

Again, what's up with this Chris guy? I could feel my ego tugging as I found myself offended that no one was asking for me. By the start of service, I was certain I never wanted to hear the name *Chris* again. It's laughable now, but I stood at the back of the sanctuary with my arms crossed, mentally scowling as I scoped out the crowd trying to deduce who was the one they called Chris.

What can he possibly have going on that I don't have?

I found myself envisioning who this superhuman Adonis of a man must be—the charm of Clooney, biceps of a Hemsworth (any of the brothers will do), and the arresting good looks of a young Brad Pitt.

I bet even his breath smelled minty-fresh perfect.

The Chris conundrum went on for another month until I couldn't stand it any longer. My curiosity got the best of me and I converted into one of those, "Hey, have you seen Chris?" people. I had to lay eyes on this Chris fella myself.

I pounded the pavement across our massive campus and asked everyone I could where Chris might be located. Finally, I found someone who clued me in to the sidewalk where this uber-greeter could usually be found working his street magic. Immediately, I absconded from my reception duties and headed to the fabled Chris territory. From afar, I observed a group of folks congregated around a single human on the side-walk, and I knew I must be reaching the epicenter.

And then I saw him.

Chris was not a superhero. Chris was not a fashion-able male model with gorgeous man hair and an envi-able smile. Chris was just a regular young guy with thin arms, a slight goatee, and a pair of pink tennis shoes. Dressed in all black (minus the Nikes), he was the kind of indistinguishable person you would pass right by in the mall if you weren't paying attention.

Today, however, I was paying attention. I broke through the crowd and lobbed my accusation, "So, you're *the* Chris?"

Without saying a word, Chris hugged me. As we broke our embrace, I couldn't help but notice the joy on his face. It wasn't just some reserved, internal joy; it flowed naturally, effortlessly from him and resonated among the group. It was suddenly obvious why people clamored to be around him.

Instantly, I was forced to drop my grumpy atti-tude and smile. This moment taught me that energy is everything. It most definitely trumps how you look, the brand of clothes you wear, or if you're hip to the latest TikTok dance.

Chris laughed out loud and never answered my question. He didn't have to—in those first few moments I could already sense exactly who he was. Chris had the most amazing spirit I had ever seen in my life. This guy was on fire for God, and everything that drove him was rooted in love. As I got to know him, I became convinced that this unimposing hipster was the truest example of God's spirit personified that I had encountered on this planet.

I found out he was a carpenter and, like most twenty-three-year-olds, trying to figure out life. Our friendship grew, and I felt a calling to do something to help foster his beautiful light so that he could further bless other people. It was unique feeling for me to yearn to help someone on a very personal level, but I counted it as a sign of growth. Until then, I had been entirely focused on my own life, not anyone else's. It was this moment that made me realize the importance of a one-on-one relationship and mentorship that I strive to carry still today. I had invested in companies and charities, but this was the first time I invested in an individual. For once, I wasn't interested in a person's outer appearance; I was looking beyond that nonsense and investing in Chris's spirit.

I found out that Chris's goal was ministry. He held a true desire not just to work on the hearts of the people in our congregation on the sidewalk, but also in the pews. It was evident that he was created for that line of work. Unfortunately, the way CCV operated made it unattainable, as they would not be able to pay him a salary for the first year. As I suspected, Chris could not afford to walk away from his job for a full year. In fact, he could barely afford his bills, making the little money that he did from woodworking. I prayed on it and then proposed that he write a budget of his monthly expenses for me.

It took a couple weeks of pestering Chris to get him to put his finances on paper. I understood his hesitation, as he didn't really know anything about me other than I was Brent the Greeter from church. However, he must have sensed that I was genuine because he finally brought me the figure of $1,800.

After examining his budget, I asked my head of human resources at MOP set up my favorite greeter with a monthly stipend. Mouth agape, Chris was floored when I told him the news that I was going to support him financially for a year. More accurately, he was overjoyed that he would get to move into ministry full time. Quite frankly, I had a tough time believing I was signing off on this as well. A nagging lawsuit, divorce, and the Alabama condo project delay had greatly reduced my funds. Making grand gestures was not a smart play for me during that time, but I felt in my soul that it was exactly what I needed to do. In fact, I knew it was what I was *called* to do.

Acting on faith and leading with my heart felt amazing! It wasn't about how much I gave, it was about following my instincts and listening to God. This was a refreshing guidepost that I was moving Up and entering into a more abundant life. As I retraced my steps, I was stunned to realize how Don had unwaveringly put me exactly where God could use me, even though I thought

Don was shortchanging me. Had I said *no* to the sidewalk greeting gig or held out for a more "dignified" seat at the table, I would have likely never encountered Chris. If Chris and I had never met, he wouldn't have had the money to begin his rightful march into ministry. I was allowing myself to be a chess piece in God's plan. After feeling small for so much of my adult life, I was letting go of myself and plugging into something much bigger.

Chris crushed it. As I had expected, the elder board loved Chris as much as his sidewalk fans did. After a year on staff supported by the stipend, he was ushered into a paid position at CCV. And then, many years later in 2017, Chris felt called to start his very own church. There is no telling how many lives he's impacted throughout the years and continues to do so to this day. Chris knew exactly who he was and showed up to always do the necessary work to keep moving Up. I'm overjoyed that God blessed me to be a small part of his success story. Whether he knows it or not, Chris is certainly a part of my victory story.

The ripple effect was addictive. One small act of kindness and one tiny step of faith can be the genesis of ripples that become mighty waves to change the world. From that moment on, I realized I didn't aspire to just make an impact in my life or my community, but also to the world and the culture.

Experiencing Chris's nature and presence triggered my realization that true spiritual life is not something that happens internally. I had moved through my whole adult life always looking down at my own path and concerned solely with my well-being. The domino effect of the Chris situation taught me to take my eyes off my feet and lift my head to see those around me. I could have missed this entire experience if I hadn't finally been looking Up.

I was absorbing and budding, but it was still very difficult for me to break timeworn patterns. Frequently, like most things in life, it would be one step forward and then two diminutive steps back—and that's OK. In my case, even as I moved Up the ladder, I found myself sliding down a rung or two when times got tough again. Without a doubt, the business arena is where I struggled the most. Whereas in my personal life I had created nothing but strife and damage by doing things "my way," with MOP I found great success operating exactly how I wanted.

Back in Ohio, the racial discrimination lawsuit was still looming over me and I was fighting it tooth and nail. Al recognized that my ingrained strategy of punching through, grinding out, and getting my way just wasn't working to move this settlement forward even an inch. Perceiving the pain the legal fight was causing me, Al noted how badly the entanglement was holding me back. He recommended that I consider opening up to a different approach.

"Brent, you've got to trust me," Al said. "It is clear that these buyers are just as tired as you are. I assure you, this has gotten way bigger than they ever wanted it to be, and now their attorney is really the one running this thing."

I released a deep exhale as I realized the truth in his words. At each meeting, the would-be buyers had looked increasingly exhausted and frustrated—not only with the process, but also with the way their lawyer was handling the whole situation. Al's strategy was a gamble, but if the plaintiffs were receptive to a conversation, it could make sense.

"You've got to reach them. You've got to find a way to speak to them directly and assure them that you want to help. Sure, you want what is best for you, but you also want what's best for them. You are eager to work through this to get it settled because it's become a burden to both of you at this point."

I contemplated this for days. If I took this route, it would be the first time I'd chosen to approach a business issue with love and compassion instead of dollars and power. I believed that emotions were a weakness that most definitely did not belong in the business world. Talk about having to overcome some very personal, deeply ingrained programming.

Even though I was incredibly skeptical, I felt I had nothing to lose at this point. Even if my request fell flat on its face, I knew this was the perfect opportunity to put into practice all that I had been learning. I was going to have to dig deep and unearth that place where my empathy outpunched my fight.

I leaned heavily on Al, and he talked me through a visualization that night and then again the next morning. It was a process of prepping for how I wanted the conversation to go, how I wanted to be seen and heard, and how I wanted the buyers to feel seen and heard as well. I thoughtfully pictured how much the buyers were hurting. Just like me, they were going through the muck, and I could envision how much they must have wanted the case to end as well. After this mental exercise, I was certain they wanted the same peace and closure that I needed. I was able to put myself aside and not look at them as opponents but see them the way God does. I focused on loving them even though I was frustrated by the drawn-out proceedings.

The next morning at court, I asked their attorney if I could speak with his clients directly—something we had never done. Surprisingly, he said *yes*. The attorney uttered nothing as I addressed his client, but my empathetic demeanor must have put him off. As I began to speak with a kind tone, he simply turned his chair around. He literally had his back to us for the remainder of the meeting. If I hadn't already been mentally prepared, that 180-degree spin would have been met with some fiery resistance by me.

Recalling my visualizations and focused on compassion, I took the opportunity to make my point clear. I said in a very calm voice, "We can fight for another year, but here's the bottom line. You walked down the hill and told me this wasn't going to work out. Please understand that my business is my life and has been my family's life for more than four decades. You were getting ready to move into my family's old house and already had a huge problem with the noise. As neighbors, we were putting ourselves in a terrible predicament. Now, I couldn't shut down my shop, but I was willing to pay you $150,000 to find another place where you could find some quiet. It would have cost you nothing, but you chose to sue me. Furthermore, you questioned my character when we both know the color of your skin had nothing to do with my decision. That's just not the way this should be."

The would-be buyer was quiet. In fact, so was his lawyer...for once. Seeing the slightest relaxation of the buyer's face, I continued, "We need to settle this, or it could go on for a long, long time. The next step goes to federal court for a Civil Rights case. Is that really what this is about?"

I could tell by the buyer's silence that he was strongly considering my words. His lawyer must have felt it as well because he rotated back around to give his client some stern advice. It was evident to all parties that the lawyer wanted to stay the course at all costs and chase the biggest payday.

We settled out of court hours later. I got to keep the house. In fact, I still own it to this day. More importantly, I learned an invaluable lesson about my ego and how much that nasty sense of self-importance was running the show. When I opened up to a different mindset and didn't try to force my will, things actually worked out for the better. Instead of charging in and fighting to the death, I saw that there was a way to communicate my intentions differently. I fully admit that initially I thought using kindness and altruism would be regarded as flaws of vulnerability that would saddle me in a position of powerlessness. In reality, the court case was concrete proof that the better way to achieve my goals (both in life and business) was to tackle each moment with fairness, calmness, and intentionality.

It's baffling that in professional sports (especially golf), a mental coach is viewed as a perfectly acceptable member of an athlete's team. But when it comes to life, people scoff at the notion. Yet how much exponentially more important is the ultimate game known as life? Why wouldn't you choose to have every competitive advantage available? I'm comfortable admitting that I need all the help I can get to remain mindful and stave off my ego from commandeering my thoughts and decisions.

With my head Up and heart open, I was working hard on my business and on bettering myself. Tom, my trainer, pointed out that even though I was improving the balancing act of my life, I seldom did anything for my personal enjoyment. I hadn't really considered that, but he was right. I decided it was time to make a change.

Now in my late forties, I had been a truck owner my entire life. I loved fast cars, but I'd always needed a truck for work. A truck made total sense because I had always viewed myself as someone who didn't deserve to enjoy life. I can't fully explain why I believed that, but I knew it to be true. Maybe subconsciously I let the shame and guilt over my failures overrule the joy of my victories. But in Phoenix, the way I treated myself was evolving, so I bought a black convertible Porsche Carrera. Call it a midlife crisis if you want, but I'm not sure if that is descriptive enough. As you've read in my story, I had been battling a whole life crisis! Besides, my mind still wouldn't let me *totally* splurge, so I got a used car. To be honest, it really paid off mentally. I felt happier than I had in years as I whipped through those mountains with my radio up, getting browned by the sun and breathing fresh air.

The real triumph is discovering what makes you happy and celebrating any place you can find it. The concept of self-worth went far beyond treating myself to a used convertible. I was becoming more mindful of self-worth in my life as a whole. It's perfectly OK to indulge ourselves in behaviors that are wholesome and good for our minds, bodies, and spirits. Reward yourself when you can. Don't punish yourself.

This doesn't mean things will be perfect; I don't think they ever will be. For me, it meant I was headed in the right direction and continuing to find the signposts to guide me along the way. Without continuing to look Up, I would have never understood how important it was for me to break the cycle of self-imposed negativity and embrace the positive in order to progress.

Chapter 8

TALKING AT THE
MAN UPSTAIRS

*A*rizona had turned out to be exactly what I needed. Once I decided on that change of scenery, the pieces seemed to fall into place. Al brought my mindset into a better mental space and helped me with meditations and visualizations. Tom brought me a better understanding of fitness, core strength, and how to care for my health. Christ Church of the Valley, its elders, and Pastor Don helped me develop my spiritual side. Within a short period of time, I had been presented with guides who fed my mind, body, and soul.

To achieve balance in your life, your mind, body, and soul have to be aligned. You cannot excel in one area and hope it makes up for the other two. It takes all three areas to prop one another up. Even if I had the most positive mental attitude in the world, if I felt horribly every day because I was abusing my physical body, I wouldn't move Up. If my health were pristine but I was not feeding my soul, I wouldn't be connected to my greater purpose. Whether it is the challenges of society, the struggles from our own emotional states, or just trying to survive everyday life, there is always something lurking to knock our focus off-kilter. I knew how much work I had ahead of me, and in order to be connected to my body, mind, and soul, it was going to require hammering my daily routine or my progress would slip away.

My early months at Christ Church of the Valley were the beginning of building my functional faith as well as assembling a team of people around me who were supportive, encouraging, and kind. As important as each of their individual contributions was to my life, complete healing is about synergy. It was the combination of the people with whom God had gifted me along the way that helped me continue to progress.

Mac McElroy is distinctively special, and we had developed a close relationship since our introduction months ago. No matter what is going on in Mac's life, you always receive his complete attention when you are in his presence. Not only does he continually know the right questions to ask to get you on track, but he is an unending supply of positivity. The more he treated me like a son, the more I looked to him as a father figure. It took our unique relationship for me to realize how much I'd missed having a paternal presence in my life since my own dad had passed away. Mac leads by actions. He doesn't need to tell you how it is with lofty words and flowery prose; you only need to examine his lifestyle to want to be more like him. Mac's intimate relationship with God fueled my curiosity to dig deeper into my own faith.

Praying wasn't a problem for me, and I found myself talking *at* God constantly throughout my day. However, it soon became clear that my communication with the Man Upstairs was less a conversation and more of an onslaught of Brent blabberings. I never took the time to be quiet and listen to God. I was so conditioned to do all the speaking by my alpha-maleness as a business leader that I hadn't really considered the value of clearing my mind to listen. With new tools from my mental coach, Al, I was able to unclutter my mind and listen to what God was calling me to do next.

It's hard to hear God over all the commotion and din in our lives and in the world. I guess I always thought if God spoke to me, I would see a burning bush like Moses. Certainly, God would recognize to whom He was talking and offer a grand gesture of sorts. Then I read 1 Kings 19:12, where the prophet Elijah expects to hear God's voice in an earthquake and then in a fire. Those don't happen, but when Elijah quiets, he finally hears God's voice *in a whisper*. That blew my mind! The Bible is literally telling us if we are open and receptive, God is so close to us that He chooses to communicate with a whisper. The Creator of the universe talks to us all the time, but we need to be still enough to hear His voice within the whisper. Ask yourself: how still are you right now in your life? Can you allow yourself to be quiet enough to hear His whisper?

When I really connected with God, my outlook on life began to shift dramatically. Gone were the days when I worried that I wouldn't make it to see age fifty. I sensed hope and I saw change. However, just like most things, as time progressed I slipped back into my old routine, and my walk with Christ became just that—routine.

If we really want to live the abundant life, we can't simply go through the motions and expect results. If we want to feel alive, it's important to do as many responsible things as we can to make us feel that way. Too many times we are afraid or feel guilty pursuing things that make us happy. It is not selfish; it is necessary. During my second winter in Phoenix, I decided to pick up my golf clubs again. Whether because of lack of time or health, I hadn't played the game I used to love in more than eight years. No more. I was seeing the results of my healing, and I wanted to revisit the things that had brought joy into my life.

A round of golf is never just a round of golf. Sure, there's the sport of it, but of equal value is the camaraderie, jokes, political debates, and the quintessential side bet on the game. I was kindly warned to watch out for Pastor Don, who played every hole as if it were the Masters and millions of dollars were at stake. So saying *yes* to play in a foursome with him one sunny afternoon was done so with the thought, *Challenge accepted.*

We decided on a two-dollar wager.

The money didn't matter. Don was my kind of guy. He was a competitor. Fortunately for me, he was also an average golfer. Unfortunately for me, he played with the intensity of Tiger Woods at all times. His game day tactics weren't limited to superior club selection or some special *Happy Gilmore* swing. No, Don's modus operandi was psychological warfare. If Don were playing golf with the leader of SEAL Team Six, he would be able to identify that man's weakness and use it to his advantage.

Over the prior twelve months, he and I had formed a brotherly friendship. We were constantly pushing each other to be better in all spheres of life—mental, physical, and, most importantly, spiritual. He was both my Paul and Timothy, my mentor and encourager. He knew the best way to motivate me was competition, and he was smart enough to use that against me!

We had an expectedly fierce game going as we approached the flag on the 18th hole of Ironwood Golf

Course. Par three. Don's drive ended up on the far left side of the green. More accurately, it was *very* far left; his ball was stuck in the fringe. Lining up the shot, Don was a solid fifty feet from the hole. Even though there was no way he would even get close with a putt, the vicious determination on his face was downright comical. I was sitting pretty with a fifteen-foot birdie putt and was positive that, minus an act of God, Don could make par at best.

The parting of the Red Sea. Jesus feeding the five thousand. Don hitting this shot. All three miracles of roughly equal possibility.

Don was playing the part and going through the normal motions of any professional golfer before trying to sink a fifty-foot putt. He checked the grain and slope— uphill and angled in a way that made the shot exponentially more difficult than just the distance. After gathering all the necessary information and calculations, he stepped up to the ball. Matching his eyes to the line, he prepared the backswing. He then, strangely, paused as he was getting ready to stroke the ball. "When I make this putt, Brent, you're going to rededicate your life to Jesus Christ."

This is what I would call a full-stop, record-scratch moment. Minutes before, Don and I had been slapping each other on the backs and pouring on the good-natured trash talk. Now Don was calling out this impossible putt and tying it to my faith? I laughed and looked at my teammate Mac for acknowledgement that this was a joke, but I received no such confirmation. Mac only gave me the same beautiful, supportive smile he seemed to always give me when I looked to him for confirmation. As I looked back at Don, he was not laughing either. Suddenly, the heaviness of his wager landed on me. He was serious. The competition was no longer important. He really believed he was going to sink an impossible shot.

Pick your favorite professional golfer, and I assure you they would be lucky to make this putt one out of two hundred, maybe three hundred, times. Don was not a pro. Don was not even what I would call *good*. Don was pedestrian at best, but something about the confidence of his words got my attention.

"Brent, are you all-in, or are you half-in and half-out?"

I realized that Don making this shot had absolutely nothing to do with our game. He knew my competitive nature and had met me where I would be open to him—the golf course. Don recognized I was still growing mentally and physically every day, but my faith journey had become complacent in a spiritual holding pattern. While I worked out and practiced meditating daily, I felt that just showing up on Sundays was good enough to strengthen my relationship with God. I didn't think I needed to do much more than that, but Don saw through my exterior and wanted me to truly tap into a spiritual awakening.

I watched as he went back to the ball and resumed lining up his putt. I annoyingly edged closer to the cup as Don circled his ball like a bird of prey. It was obvious the stakes were no longer the two-dollar bet as he looked at the shot from every conceivable angle. He felt the grass and then the weight of the putter in his hands. I watched the small backstroke, and then Don gently tapped the ball with an anticlimactic *clink*.

I tracked the wayward white sphere as it embarked on its hopeless journey.

Fifty ... forty ... thirty ... twenty ... ten ...

As it neared the cup, I can only assume a miniature black hole vortex briefly formed directly over the hole on this particular course smack-dab in the middle of Anthem, Arizona. Don's ball was sucked straight into the cup.

He didn't say a word.

Needless to say, I didn't make my easy putt to tie our game. It might sound silly, but I was too shaken up by what I had just experienced. Typically, I don't take losing well. This game should have been no different, but it felt different.

Very different.

I had just witnessed a minor miracle by a holy man invoking the direction of my life. It was too crazy, too unlikely, to be written off as randomness, and I can assure you it had nothing to do with Don's skill as a golfer. The more I wrestled with it, the more apparent it became that all these "chance" events in my life weren't so random at all. All of the things that had happened to me with seemingly no connection were billboards leading me to this moment. The signs had been all around me—guideposts from God—but my head had been down as I focused solely on my work and myself. Now, with my eyes open and my mind and heart yearning for something different, something better, some-thing more fulfilling, I could make out patterns of the perceived randomness and realize it was all happening because I mattered. I had value. People like Don knew that I mattered. God knew that I mattered. *I* needed to know that I mattered.

That's a hard lesson to accept in our lives. Our brains can understand the theory of self-value, but our hearts can blindly lag behind. Even when we begin to *know* we have value, it's a struggle to *feel* like we have value. It may not happen in the same way for you as it did for me, but if you're looking Up and paying attention, the signs will present themselves. Again, it's your unique journey, and it's specifically laid out for you to discover for yourself.

Take a moment and put down this book so you can spend a few minutes meditating on your past. Challenge yourself to find the "random" events that were critical to getting you where you are in this moment. Across the spectrum of subtleness, key events and people have shaped you into becoming a better version of yourself. You have to be open, focus on the present, and believe enough in yourself to know that you're worth it. Many times, it comes through pain and struggle at first. Yet if you can find the lesson in the turmoil and stay positive, it will turn into growth and eventually flow into abundance. It's worth hearing me say it again—you matter.

One of the biggest things this self-work has taught me is that we can't sit idly by and expect God to force us to change. For most of my life, that was exactly how I operated. I prayed and simply expected good things to happen. I never put myself in the proper mindset to actually pursue God. If you love someone, you pursue them. In fact, God demonstrated that by sending an army to reach me—Mac, Don, Al, Tom, and others—because that's how much I mattered to Him. I'm a hardheaded guy, so the Lord knew He would have to keep on sending the people before I would listen. That's the beauty of God; if you keep your eyes open, you will find Him pursuing you!

As I got healthier so did my perspective, and instead of merely sitting around waiting for God to help me, I fundamentally changed my prayers into what I call *active prayers*. With the proper energy and proactiveness, I wanted to become a bigger part of the solution. I incorporated my meditation into my prayer routine and was able to shift my energy to feel differently. As I breathed in oxygen, I focused deeply on whomever or whatever I was praying about. As I exhaled, I envisioned sending my love and compassion to the subjects of my prayers. Suddenly my prayer life became so laser-focused that, not only was I asking my Creator to help and intercede, but I also began to feel like an involved partner. The connection was holistic and physical. Thus, the name *active prayer*. It may sound silly and only seem like a subtle change, but it made a massive difference for me in my conversations with God.

Megachurches attract guest speakers like moths to the proverbial flame. For all the negatives lobbed against large congregations, the variety of big-name faith influencers who come through the doors to take the stage is truly special. Throughout the years, I've been on the receiving end of countless sermons and have attended my fair share of professional association dinners with lauded speakers. I've been inspired by many of these fine orators, but I've never found one who was able to motivate me to really put my faith into action.

Author Barry Cameron changed all of that.

Author of *Contagious Generosity: The Key to Continuous Blessing!*, Barry visited us at CCV from Grand Prairie, TX, deep in the heart of the Lone Star State. I had heard Barry speak once before in the middle of the 2008 banking crisis. His message of radical giving had many in the congregation wincing. Folks were out of work and scraping just to get by, and here was this crazy Texan urging us to give generously. Needless to say, at that snapshot in time, I was totally unprepared and unavailable to let his words permeate.

Now Barry was back with a similar challenge as he assured us that we were not as charitable as we could be. This sentiment from his book sums up the content of his sermon:

> *Because when we are generous, we are more like God. That's why it feels so good whenever we do it. Whenever and wherever we are generous, it always feels good, always feels right, and rightly so. That's the way generosity is. Generosity reflects the character of God.*[2]

The longer Barry spoke, the more my initial misgivings peeled back and his message resonated. Barry introduced the story of Vertrue Sharp, a preacher from Maryville, Tennessee. He was a penny-wise man who saved every hard-earned dollar. Many thought him to be miserly. He was a tireless worker, and when he wasn't preaching, he was raising cattle and growing hay on his seventy-three-acre farm.[3] When Pastor Sharp died at the ripe old age of ninety-four, he had quietly amassed a two-million-dollar estate. He had worked for that money his entire life but never spent any of it on himself. Truthfully, he never worked for *money*; it was evident that he worked for *God*. This selfless man's will mandated that every last cent be given away to several hospitals and seven different charities.

A story of that magnitude has a way of making you feel very, very small, and I've always abhorred that feeling. However, this time I was feeling "less than" for the right reason. Deep down, I knew I wasn't maximizing what I could do with my business. My biggest financial leap of faith up to that moment had been providing for Chris so he could be a part of CCV's ministry. Surely that was important, but was I honestly giving enough compared to what I had been given? Even that thought was a novel idea. Before my spiritual awakening, everything I had was mine because I had worked for it. I'd busted my butt. I'd made it all happen. But the ego-driven clouds of my mind were parting, and I'd realized money wasn't mine because I'd earned it. It was only given to me because it was to be a blessing:

> Command those who are rich in this present world
> not to be arrogant nor to put their hope in wealth,
> which is so uncertain, but to put their hope in God,
> who richly provides us with everything for our

enjoyment. *Command them to do good, to be rich in good deeds, and to be generous and willing to share.* In this way they will lay up treasure for themselves as a firm foundation for the coming age, so that they may take hold of the life that is truly life (1 Timothy 6:17–19 NIV, emphasis mine).

Barry took the ideas in these verses and expanded them: "I am convinced when you and I begin giving more, God will bless us with more, and we'll have more to give."[4] That summation was all it took. Literally, Barry finished his sermon and I was ready to rock 'n' roll. The motto "make more, save more, give more" was instantly burned into my thoughts.

I marched out of church with those six simple words that I believed redefined my sense of purpose and attitude toward money. Everything immediately became clear, and I sat down to strategize as soon as I got home. I wanted this motto to distinguish my life. I could take baby steps or . . .

I could dive headfirst into the deep end.

I kept things extremely simple. The fewer possessions I owned, the easier it would be for me to be grateful and generous to those around me. The only things I needed daily to do were wake up, put on my clothes, and evolve. As I found peace from shaking loose my material trappings, I received an even bigger, more bizarre calling. It made so little sense that I concluded it could only be a thought put in my head by God Himself. In order to fully embrace my newfound mindset, I felt certain I had to move back to Ohio.

Whoa.

It was time to leave the healing and comfort I'd found in Arizona and move back to the city that had almost taken my life. I was called to reengage with my business and family on a whole new, healthy level. I wagered that I was now a person who could operate with a healthy balance between the two. Heading back into the belly of the beast, I was confident I would be able to handle it with my newly learned techniques and practices. There was a risk that I might lose all the momentum I had gained in Arizona and go back to the "old me," as Pendleton still was definitely not my happy place. But I knew the next step in my journey was to make it my happy place.

The next week, I called a Realtor and put my new Scottsdale house on the market. Then I gifted my beloved Porsche convertible to the church so they could sell it and put the proceeds toward good work. Before I left, I started funding a special church account for Mac with $30,000 to $40,000 each year. He could use that money to cut through red tape to help bless people who needed help. Wherever there is a need, Mac provides a blessing. I'm not going to lie; I have also been extremely blessed as Mac shares the amazing stories of hope with me.

With this contagious generosity, my soul was soaring. The more I gave, the lighter my soul became, and the higher I could fly. Unshackled, there was no doubt I was undeniably headed Up. I knew my purpose was to bring as many as I could with me!

And you can say what is, or fight for it
Close your mind or take a risk
You can say it's mine and clench your fist
Or see each sunrise as a gift
We're going to get it, get it together right now
Going to get it, get it together somehow
Going to get it, get it together and flower
We're going to get it, get it together I know
Going to get it, get it together and flow
Going get it, get it together and go
Up and Up and Up.

Up & Up
Words and Music by Christopher Martin, William Champion,
Jonathan Buckland, Guy Berryman, Tor Hermansen and
Mikkel Eriksen
Used by permission.

Chapter 9

LEARNING TO WALK THE WALK

I was optimistically ecstatic but still wise enough to know that plugging back into my old life without a grounded routine was a grade-A plan for disaster. If I were going to keep up my success, I had to have a crystal-clear system that kept me moving Up in my growth. In order to push through any unproductivity, I would need to work on all three pillars of mind, body, and soul. To me, this was the key to all-encompassing spirituality. If I wanted to stay rooted, I couldn't *only* do the work when I felt like it or if I were struggling. Like an alcoholic returning to a drink, my natural programming was always bubbling under the surface, waiting for pressures and stresses to dip me back into my old, dangerous ways. It's as if we always have an angel and a demon on our shoulders, and if we aren't actively listening to God, then the devil wins by default. As humans, we are simply too weak on our own not to follow our carnal instincts and ultimately make bad decisions. Oftentimes, *really* bad decisions . . .

This is what we are all competing against every day. If we really want to change our thoughts, behaviors, feelings, and emotions permanently, we have to create enough new daily actions to make it happen. There is a reason professional athletes still have to practice every day to excel at their sports. You would think that being the best in the world would mean that these players could get away without honing their skills daily. The bigger truth is, it is not just a sport for these players. It doesn't matter if you're Brady or LeBron—to stay at the top of your game, daily practice has to become a lifestyle if you truly desire real success.

I evaluated the things that had shifted me in a positive direction during my rebuilding process in Arizona. After identifying the practices that would lead me to continued success, I built a distinct routine around them. I keep it simple. I've found that the more complicated you make a regimen, the more likely you can convince yourself to skip it.

It is extremely important that the first thing you should do in the morning is start with the two Gs—gratitude and God. I can confidently tell you that how you choose to begin your day will set you up for success or push you in the direction of failure. I want to think about something greater than me, so I begin my day by reading my Bible.

Next, I focus on connecting to my breath and my body. Making sure I have correct posture, I sit with my feet flat on the floor. Being grounded allows me to breathe into the crown of my head to activate the back of my brain. If I have any emotional or physical issues, I send energy to those areas. I move from there into active prayer where I calm myself and listen to God. With that kind of energy flowing through me, I think about all the people in my life and how grateful I am to be in their worlds. Finally, I visualize how I want to be present in all of my activities for the day. As I open my eyes, I feel completely clear and ready to tackle my day.

With my mind at ease, I progress to getting my body active. It's crucial for me to get moving by hitting the gym, doing stretches at home, or going for a hike. The rest of my day is spent living mindfully—and that includes what I eat. I focus on eating foods that are going to honor it and avoid eating out of emotion.

Some days the routine was more challenging than others as human fragility kicked in and motivation ebbed and flowed. Early morning work meetings weren't much help either.

The first part of my mantra was *make more*, and in order to do that, I soon felt the familiar pull of MOP. For better or worse, I threw myself back into work, and it was a little bumpy.

I was dealing with people in my business and personal lives who had known me and my old programmed ways for a lifetime. I'm sure they didn't know what to expect of the new Brent, and I was self-conscious as I didn't want people to think that I had lost my mind in Phoenix. Since I was still slowly transitioning to living and leading more mindfully, I knew to tread lightly and reengage by dipping my toe in the water. That meant listening and observing as much as I was talking and directing. I also felt it was important to reconnect with the guys in the field and let them know that I was present for them. I just had to remind myself to keep practicing. If you want to get better at guitar, you practice. If you want to learn to speak Spanish, you practice. If you want to get better at life, you practice your routine. There is no other way.

It didn't take long for the first test to come my way at MOP. After a few months back, I got an unusual text from Bob, one of my higher-level employees. Now, Bob and I were friendly, but we weren't friends. I thought it was odd that Bob was eager to grab lunch, but my curiosity was piqued.

Bob wasted no time. As soon as the waitress took our drink orders, he nervously said, "We've got a problem. Steven is trying to undermine your business and you." This raised a giant red flag—a drenched-in-gasoline-bursting-with-flames red flag. Not only was Steven a trusted employee; more importantly, he was a friend.

By the time the waitress returned with my Arnold Palmer, I was in total shock. Bob talked through a detailed list of eight or nine accusations concerning Steven. Obviously, I didn't want to believe this was happening right under my nose or behind my back. I hoped the claims were false, and I'd decided to reserve my thoughts until I heard Steve's side. Taking this breather was something the Old Brent would not have done. With a hurt ego, I would have gone after Steve like a raging bull. However, after suffering through an unfounded lawsuit and a nasty divorce, I'd learned there are always two sides to every story.

Bob felt strongly about Steve and didn't want to show the same patience I did. In fact, after his litany of offenses, he gave me a firm ultimatum: either I fired Steve or Bob would leave.

I felt the rapid speed of my thoughts jolt into gear and send my brain spiraling. Bob was a stellar employee for MOP, but he seemed to be leveraging his knowledge to get his own way. At this point in my business, I felt every employee was critical to the organization, and I didn't want to lose anyone. I simply couldn't afford it.

I took a much-needed deep breath to slow things down and create a quiet mind and some space to think. Once I was able to wrangle and control my runaway thoughts, my mental training told me to hit the pause button altogether. This ability is a powerful tool in any boss's kit. Every decision does not have to be made on the spot, and it is incumbent on you to dictate the tempo of your conversations if you want to maintain control. I thanked Bob and assured him I would look into these matters. It was not the immediate answer he was looking for, but I didn't want to be rash or hasty. High-stress moments such as these can be overwhelming, so slowing things down helps to create some peaceful moments for quiet time.

That very night, I started digging into Bob's accusations and found out that some of the allegations had merit while other claims appeared to come down to operational subjectivity. For now, I had to judiciously weigh the options. I had to be mindful about the next steps because no matter what decision I made, I was going to lose a significant employee. MOP was at a critical crossroads, and I was worried that an internal investigation could quickly devolve into a witch hunt that would rattle our team and ripple through my company. The odds were that stirring this pot unnecessarily would make things much, much worse.

Furthermore, the pipeline industry leadership positions had been at capacity for the last year. There was little time or chance to woo someone away from a different outfit and get them settled as we were flooded with projects. If I fired Steve, I would not be able to fill his shoes; there was literally no one available. I was firmly wedged between a rock and a hard place.

After considering every aspect and ramification, I decided that Steve's infractions didn't justify an all-hands-on deck implosion. After an in-depth conversation with Steve, I called Bob to let him know my final decision. Bob understood and instantaneously gave his two-week notice. He hadn't been bluffing about his ultimatum and, to be honest, I respected that. I asked Bob if he would work with me a little longer to ensure an orderly transition with his replacement. After all, Bob was crucially involved with our customers, workforce, and processes. Bob seemed grateful and said he would reconsider.

The next thing I knew, Bob vanished into thin air.

I later found out that he had quickly taken a job with a geothermal drilling company. The contacts in that industry are completely different from those in the natural gas world, so I counted my blessings that Bob wouldn't be a competitor. I was eager to put the drama aside and close the chapter on that book.

Except that chapter refused to stay closed—not even a little. Bob had been well liked at MOP and had spent the last two years buddying up to all my employees. A week after Bob left, I lost fifteen employees. Just like Bob, they pulled Houdinis. Without any notice, these workers simply stopped showing up to jobsites. At that time, MOP only had fifty employees. Total. Essentially, a third of my office evaporated almost overnight. I fought through the turmoil and did my best to recruit replacements. After a week, I slowly got control of the reins on the situation when there was finally a lull in employees leaving for other opportunities. However, that was short-lived. Three more workers suddenly gave their notice, and the following week, a couple more left. My business had been crippled in just one month.

Stressful does not have the scope or weight to adequately describe the impact my company's free fall had on me. We were hitting terminal velocity. We were plummeting straight down at a speed that would kill the company. Needless to say, this was one of the most delicate times in my company's history.

Strangely, I felt different than I expected; I was energized. I actually felt stronger. The pressure felt ... manageable.

My daily routine of staying centered and balanced was proving to pay huge dividends. Instead of suffering from dread and despair, I stayed rested and recharged. I was walking the walk of my work, and it was paying off in my health. Don't get me wrong; I was still emotionally triggered and I knew I had to fight to save my company.

Replacing our decimated crew became paramount, and we were losing that war. My worst fears were realized when there were no immediate replacements to be found in Ohio. As a stopgap fix, I loaded up all our subcontractors with the work we couldn't handle. To further make ends meet, we rented our equipment to other companies when it wasn't being used on jobsites. I still had that puncher's mentality in me, and I would not be stopped by a former employee's attempted coup.

But the Old Brent was gone, and I was going to fight differently this time.

While battling to figure out how to keep the business afloat, I decided to check with the state of Ohio to see if Bob had started a new business, and indeed he had. As I aggregated the info, the picture became very apparent. I learned that Bob had convinced his new water drilling company to get into the natural gas business. Bob had become a part owner in that business. This meant Bob had not only taken my employees, he had been taking my customers too. And while he was working for me, he had tried to get Steve fired to put his new company in a better position. This had officially turned into a dogfight.

Immediately I scheduled a meeting with the president of Bob's new company, ABC Drilling. Our conversation went nowhere as he denied taking my people. To be honest, I actually had no reference point of how many of my employees had moved over to ABC. It was pure conjecture on my part, but I did know the mysterious exodus had begun with Bob's departure. Without any hard data, I was stuck in neutral with my accusations against ABC. Then everything changed due to one errant email.

Out of the blue, Payroll Workers Comp, a compliance company, inadvertently sent all of ABC's employee names and contact information to our office. I quickly matched names and learned that thirty of my former employees had gone to work for them. That list is what I call a literal godsend, and I was extremely grateful.

ABC was a big, deep-pocketed outfit that had been in business for about thirty years. Do you know how much that mattered to me? Zero. It was just another

David versus Goliath battle for me. I was smaller, but hungrier. I was prepared to scrap for my company until the bitter end. I scheduled another meeting with the president of ABC.

I wondered if he thought he had me by the hooks with my crumbling business. Maybe he anticipated I was here to sell MOP at a discounted rate? Or offer some type of alliance out of my position of weakness? Truth is, I didn't even let him get a question out of his grinning mouth before I told him exactly how the situation was about to play out.

"Here's what's going to happen. You are going to get loaded up with work in the natural gas field. Then, personally, I am going to show up on your jobsites to hire every guy you have."

Somewhere between a chortle and a laugh, he retorted, "How exactly do you plan on doing that?"

"I'll offer higher wages," I countered with a faux sense of confidence, knowing ABC had much, much more cash on hand.

He argued, "I'll just raise my rates and get them back."

"You can do that, but this is how it will turn out. I am going to stand in this fight for a long time. I will play the wage raise game, but the difference is, it will get high enough that you won't want to operate. I am the one who is going to make money in this scenario because I know how to operate a gas business *efficiently*. You and your team don't have a clue how to run a gas operation. Your margins will be shot, and you will have to continually raise your rates and bids to keep up until it no longer makes sense for you or your customers. And by the way, Bob is in marketing. Bob couldn't read a gas bill, much less run a natural gas division."

"We'll see," the president replied coolly.

But I wasn't backing down. "In the end, you take one more person of mine, and we will both be losers. But I will go out knowing I gave it my best. You will go out not being able to fulfill contracts, and you'll lose bigger than me. Think about it. You haven't built a team that can make things happen yet."

"You don't even know who I have on the team. Much less what they're capable of." He straightened in his chair to exude an air of self-assuredness.

Man, was this the moment I had been waiting for!

With a smile, I rattled off the names of the employees he had poached. He was uninterested. But this is where it got even sweeter.

"I know every employee on your roster. I have their phone numbers, addresses, and emails."

He laughed at what he could only assume was my puffed-up bluff. Then I pulled out the list from payroll and started with *Adams, Phil* and made it down through the Fs before he realized the severity of the situation. His demeanor changed quickly. As he picked his jaw up off his desk, I said, "I know you've got seventy-five guys. You take one more person from MOP or one more customer, and I am going to show up on your jobsites."

Then I walked out of his office.

I never again had another employee leave for ABC Drilling. In fact, I was so concrete in my conversation with the president that I assure you, if one of my employees had even reached out to them for employment, he would have turned them down. The truth is, he didn't want any part of me. But the truth behind that truth is, if he had called me out and escalated the battle, I would have been dead in the water. After my 2008 year—the lawsuit, my divorce, and the financial crisis—I did not have the capital for a fight. I'm grateful I landed the one-punch knockout just like my old man had. If we had gone twelve rounds, I would have lost that match ten times out of ten.

Here's the great thing about healing: the facets of your life and personality that used to dominate you in negative ways can now be wrangled to be used in a positive manner. I still had the same traits that had made me a good leader when I was the Old Brent, but the new me was capable of taking those characteristics and using them in a healthy manner. So even though I sounded hotheaded and came in with bravado, I handled it better than the old me would have. I didn't work off a hurt or bruised ego. Instead, I was centered and calm. By not becoming emotionally overwhelmed, I had total peace during the process.

Some days this work will be a game of inches, and if you handle things only a shade better than you did the day before, that is a victory. At other times, you may feel like you gained a mile. Whether you're taking giant leaps or small steps, as long as you are growing, you are winning. This process takes patience. You will find those moments that feel like the proverbial "two steps back" when you make a mistake or tap back into your old programming. Without a doubt, setbacks are bound to happen.

That brings up another huge component of this work—grace. Never be too hard on yourself. We are humans. Fallible. Irritable. Confused. It's like the old adage says, "It's not how many times you get knocked down, it's how many times you get back up." There is it again—*Up!* And remember, Up is a direction, not a speed.

While I was relishing my ABC Drilling victory, my company was still gutted. We limped along for the rest of 2010 and drifted for most of 2011. I stayed focused on keeping the business viable while praying to exhume some options that would lead to better financial days. With our net revenue seemingly on autopilot, and the company unable to grow, I had no idea how to get us *unstuck*.

My plan of "make more, save more, give more" was withering. I began to seriously doubt my whole crazy idea of pushing away what I'd had in Arizona to come back East. Continually, I had to remind myself to stay grateful or I could backslide to Old Brent at any moment. Even at low times when I felt defeated, I stayed in my routine of active prayer, positive mental programming, and intense daily fitness. I had to quiet myself amidst the chaotic work environment around me to listen to God, as He was the One who had brought me back to Ohio. Once I listened to His whisper, I was confident that, with faith, great things were around the corner. Even in the darkest moments, you just have to keep moving through the messy parts to see the sun again.

In late 2011, at the height of my despair, fracking came to Ohio, Pennsylvania, and West Virginia. My business exploded.

People go where there are jobs, and seemingly overnight, thousands of individuals migrated to Ohio looking for work. With the flood of new business, mass hiring couldn't happen fast enough, and we were on these new workers as soon as they hit the border. At the apex of craziness, I had to book hotel banquet rooms to have enough space to interview hundreds of people to fill seventy-five positions. There were hiring cycles where the only prerequisite for prospects was the ability to pass a drug test. They didn't know us, and we did not know them, but they got the job. The hypersonic pace at which this industry was moving meant no time for training. The only learning would be hands-on, trial by fire in the thick of the jobsite.

Furthermore, there was no time to orient new hires to our corporate culture. We dumped them straight into the field to deliver on customer expectations and pull off the job in a timely manner. Our business at MOP doubled every year for five consecutive years. That incredible fracking run took us from our depleted twenty employees all the way to a five-hundred-person workforce!

As things burst into full swing and we were doing everything we could to keep up, I had to be especially mindful not to slump back into old habits. My daily routines were still solid, but I found myself missing my mentors back in Phoenix. I was able to call them when I needed support, but it wasn't the same as being there. I realized the next step in my process would be to create deliberate connections with positive people in Ohio. The place where I was lacking the most was my soul, and I desperately needed some roots to stay grounded.

In early 2013, Jordan invited me to go to the Final Four in New Orleans for a father-son trip. Family had become increasingly important to me, and I knew it was moments like these that I had longed for with my own father. Being with my son, my soul was stirring. I was elated that we were being proactive before it was too late.

While we were there, one of Jordan's friends, Cole Patchell, invited us to an Athletes in Action (AIA) breakfast. Serving, training, and preparing athletes to be faith influencers in the world is the organization's prime objective. By building spiritual movements through the platform of sport, AIA hopes to make it so everyone knows at least one person on every team in every sport who truly follows Jesus. My interest was immediately piqued as AIA merges two worlds that I loved—athletics and faith.

The rousing messages from the passionate speakers inspired me to grab a volunteer form on the table in front of me. I didn't waste any time filling it out, even though the easier action would have been to write a check and walk away. It would have been perfect with all the success I was having in business since I was "making more, saving more," and this was my chance to start giving more again. But I wanted something deeper. I was motivated by my faith to be active and not simply a dollar sign.

An engaged faith is something my younger self would have never considered, but AIA became a kickoff point for me. As I was growing in my faith, I was becoming more aware of the problems beyond my myopic bubble out in the larger world. It became clearer and clearer that my greater purpose was to help others. AIA convinced me that it doesn't only take money to make a difference. With God, the prerequisites for one to be used for the greater good are few. All it takes is one look at the flawed Bible heroes to realize that with faith, an open heart, and the right mindset, you can move mountains. You might not have the money, but you may have the time, expertise, or brainpower that can help change the world. The best part is that you don't have the laborious task of transforming *the whole earth*; even when you help just one person, the world feels your impact.

Once I focused on an active faith mindset, I could kill two birds with one stone by spending my valuable time to make more money, which would allow me to ultimately give more. Following Barry's Cameron's philosophy, I went right back into the *making more* mode, but not with MOP. I wanted to spend more time with my son, and we had just finished the last construction project together, putting in sixty condos in Columbus, Georgia. He handled almost all of it, and I had so much respect for him as a businessman. It was time to identify our next business opportunity.

I knew Jordan could accomplish anything, but I wanted to make sure that he was his own person with autonomy. Men have an innate instinct to want to do better than their fathers. I know I was always looking and positioning myself to get ahead of my old man, and it completely torpedoed our relationship. Jordan has my DNA coursing through his veins, so I was cognizant of the most effective way to nurture our relationship. I had to keep him close and busy. He was conservative and needed something stable. I knew if I didn't get the next project going as soon as possible, he would move on and find his own.

While getting a haircut one afternoon, I noticed that single hairstylists typically had individual chairs within a larger salon. The wheels started spinning, and I quizzed my hairstylist about the mechanics of the industry business model. Evidently, in the beauty industry, it's traditional for a stylist to work for a salon as an employee.

I did more trade research, conducted informal interviews, and ran some numbers to land on a real estate solution. If we partitioned a stand-alone building for stylists, we could offer them a flat fee structure based on the size of the space they rented. We would provide the infrastructure, and they would build their business within their own space. This meant they could truly make their career their own and keep 100 percent of the income. By my estimates, this would allow stylists to double or even triple their income. At the same time, as landlords we'd score solid profit based on the take between the cumulative rents of the stylists versus our monthly lease price for the whole building. It was a total win-win for all parties and a chance to elevate others. When I approached my stylist about the opportunity, my suspicions were confirmed in a big and grateful way.

I had zero idea about running salons, and that should have been very, very terrifying for someone who was about to take on a significant amount of debt to shake up that industry. However, I do know how to evaluate businesses, and you have to stick to an unwavering formula to be profitable. Is there a need? Is the return on investment realistic? Do the numbers make sense? The final and most important variable that I was considering for the very first time—does it make people's lives better? In this case, the answer was *yes* across the board. Besides, I had an ace up my sleeve: Jordan.

I got right to work on it. At first, I considered partnering with an established franchise that was building similar projects. However, Jordan convinced me that if we built this from the ground up, it would be more profitable. The safe play was to go with the franchise, but Jordan was eager to bet on us. Something about the *us* of it took away my fears. If we wanted to make the biggest splash possible, Jordan and I would have to cannonball right into the deep end. When it was all said and done, we didn't end up with one Salon Suite but four! I'm proud to say they are doing quite well and no franchise was needed. The money is great, but it is truly doing well because people's lives are changed forever. This rental model allows stylists who may have never been able to operate as individual proprietors a chance to own their businesses. More established stylists benefit by keeping a larger share of the money they make and putting it back into their business to keep their growth cycle alive. I have found great joy being a small part of making the world better, one stylist at a time. Just remember, if you honor yourself and others in business, everyone wins. Simply put, we are better together.

Chapter 10
STRIKING OUT

"*N*o man ever steps in the same river twice, for it's not the same river and he's not the same man."

Greek philosopher Heraclitus might have said this over 2,500 years ago, but it remains true to this day. If I could guarantee one thing in life, it's that life never stays the same. By mid-2013, I was not the same man I'd been. I was doing business differently, showing up with my family differently, and living my overall life differently. In my situation, different was definitively better.

MOP meant so much to me as a family business, and I was grateful for its success and abundance. With that said, I was smart enough to realize that the fracking boom's best days were not on the horizon, but in the past.

Wanting to capitalize on our most profitable years before a slowdown, I considered selling our family business ... again. While I was engaged in the company at this time, I wasn't 100 percent running the show. Unloading MOP would allow me to take my money off the table and leave the impending restructuring of the company to someone else.

Besides, this would be a fiscal windfall that would only allow me to further my mantra of "make more, save more, give more." The more I prayed and meditated about putting the company on the market, the stronger I felt about it.

Typically, the process of selling a company not only takes the investment of time and money, but also giving up control to the right broker. While pondering the best possible strategy, I was dealing with a flush of emotions surrounding the whole process. I had concerns MOP would lose its family appeal and our people wouldn't be taken care of on a personal level. If we went corporate, could MOP's legacy actually carry forward? Furthermore, once we put ourselves out there, would anyone even be interested in us? The whole procedure felt very big, and I felt very small. That insignificant feeling certainly had the ability to trigger the Old Brent. This process was going to be a harrowing one.

I was forced to relinquish more control than I was comfortable with to allow our broker to take the reins. It was weird and distressing to be stuck in the passenger seat. This was the biggest business deal of my life, and in many ways I was now relegated to the copilot position. But I pushed ahead with faith that I would be able to keep a grip on it all. It was something I had to learn the hard way, but a great leader knows when to let someone else take charge.

The process was long and arduous. In the end, one hundred prospective buyers examined us, and fourteen of them made offers. Of the fourteen, we whittled those fourteen down to six that we thought could offer a solid potential partnership. From that prospective list, we further narrowed it down to a Texas pipeline company named Strike. By January 2014, we officially had a letter of intent (LOI) to be purchased.

This started the rigorous due diligence activity. To be frank, I felt very naked as they rifled through our financials and burrowed deep into our operating systems. Processes such as human resources, safety training protocols, accounting, and payroll were torn apart and scrutinized from every conceivable angle. Because we had grown so rapidly, our back-end systems had not kept up with the extreme rate of expansion. We knew we were a little short in those departments, but I considered that to be minor stuff that was easily navigable. As their auditors further explored our company, the most pressing issues became how we found customers, priced jobs, and calculated profitability.

Being a family business, we had no official bid process when we made sales calls to meet prospective customers. We certainly had parameters, but every job was unique so nothing was formulaic. We were not automated; we looked at each job case by case. I fully comprehended that this was not ideal, but I relied on our broker and others inside the company to traverse these stickier details.

There was too much room for error in our method, and I knew it. In order to steer this discovery process in the right direction, I would have to take it back over completely. However, I was still trying to maintain my stringent balance of work and health. Taking over this task would put me back into eighty-hour workweeks. My peace had become too important, and I wasn't willing to do that—even if it meant losing out on a one-hundred-million-dollar sale.

With little surprise, Strike ultimately decided that we didn't have a formidable enough handle on our business. Furthermore, after meeting some of our employees, their confidence in us had dropped even further. Our numbers on paper were good, but the very things I knew needed changing, they saw too. After they completed their research, Strike came back with a reduced offer of 40 percent of the originally negotiated price. I wasn't surprised, but the price point had sunk to depths where it just didn't make sense to continue the conversation.

It was evident I had yielded too much power to certain employees and hadn't led fearlessly from a place of strength. Somehow I had lost that vigor and was now behaving in ways the younger me would have ridiculed. Still, I wanted to be ahead of the curve if we ever wanted to try to sell again, and that meant restructuring the culture of the company. It was time to start letting go of employees who were no longer a solid fit for MOP.

This botched sale was not a total loss because it taught me a handful of essential lessons. This is the part where I hark back to living life with no regrets, only lessons. Any failure is a guidepost for evaluation, and you have to be willing to take the teaching to move Up. Be active and evaluate what went wrong so that when an opportunity presents itself again, you will not repeat harmful patterns and programming. By assessing everything that held you back, you can make a plan to overcome those barriers in the future. My eyes were wide open to finding the silver-lining lessons within my ruined sale.

First, if you are going to sell a company, you'd better own the experience. By stepping aside, I had played the sale very small and let the whole thing quickly spiral out of hand. I needed to be 100 percent in control—and I wasn't. I also needed to have a handle on everything happening inside my company—and I didn't. When I'd been more hands-on, it was never like me to have poorly running systems or employee issues. We had outgrown our old way of doing things, and I hadn't adapted. I had a roster of dedicated employees who made up the backbone of MOP and its culture, but there were a few bad seeds that my leadership team had allowed to linger way too long.

We do this in life as well. How many bad friends or vampires do we admit into our inner circle daily— people we allow to suck the life and joy out of us? Then we let those toxic relationships chafe and masticate like a cancer. Ultimately, we will find a person's presence is detrimental to our health, but we refuse to cut them out of our lives early on. The longer we allow a poisonous relationship to fester, the harder it is to finally end it.

Secondly, don't let fear of losing an employee hold you back from making tough calls. This is more common in business than you might imagine, as owners can feel an employee is so critical to the organization that they can't run their business without them. As a result, they will let their employee's poor attitude or behavior slide. Owners will often feel they have no choice but to let this happen, even if those employees are contaminating those around them. It takes a lot of strength, courage, and faith to stand up to these types of workers. Imagine a pro baseball team with a prima donna superstar who has a terrible attitude. The coach keeps the player around because he hits monster home runs even though he brings the clubhouse morale down. The sad truth is that the coach is too afraid to play without him because his talent is placed on a pedestal high above his moral compass. However, so many times, you will see a team playing better as a whole once the prima donna is traded. Why? The poisonous attitude is gone, and the team comes together as one unit. A team working together will always beat a single player working against their own team. It's an intimidating decision (and not as easy as you might think) to fire someone who's considered a rock-star employee, but I came to understand why it's sometimes a necessity.

I took time to reflect on the whole experience and get clarity on what it all meant. I would never be able to move my company forward with employees who didn't fit or who weren't aligned with our familial mindset. Restructuring was imperative; there was no other way to move Up. If you want to travel Up, it is vital to surround yourself with people who are looking to launch in that same direction. Anyone or anything that is an anchor will only slow down your ascension, and remember— no one can hold you down!

The Strike experience highlighted other areas where we could improve and add value for a future buyer. Blowing through money, I spent the rest of that year refining our systems, processes, and safety practices. Things felt rudderless at MOP by the end of 2014 as these added expenses, coupled with a cooling energy market, left us financially flat. The wind was once again out of the company sails.

No matter how far you progress, old programming is never completely killed. You only bury it away somewhere cavernous in your psyche and hope it never comes back. Unfortunately, stress and doubt have the extraordinary ability to locate the Old You and bring up the damaging stuff in ferocious ways if you are not prepared to deal with them.

I got focused with a game-ready mindset and started changing my thoughts around the work we did. Desperate for ways to balance our financials, my strategy was to fully take over and grow the distribution side of our business. On the distribution side, we worked for utility companies running gas within the towns and cities. We were primarily a front-facing organization with the customers because we were tying gas lines from the street directly into their homes. This had always been our bread and butter. It is what MOP spent almost forty years doing prior to walking away from Columbia Gas. In order to pull off this rebuild and take the company back Up, I would have to focus all of my energy on building up the distribution side. This meant my boots would be back on the ground and on-site while leading the company as a whole. For sure, this would be the most demanding experience since my health had declined in 2008, and it would require me to be at the top of my mental, physical, and spiritual games.

With the distribution side under my full control, I expected that we would eventually grow and that progress would allow me to make moves to bring on new employees while I phased out old ones.

I soon found that resurgence was on the horizon. It wasn't financial; it was much, much more important than money. Family was not only coming back to MOP, but back into my life as a whole.

Ironically, building a family business often leads to the family suffering in the process. With all-consuming focus and pressure going into the operation, it takes you away from everything that truly matters. When you are in the thick of it as a small business owner, you typically don't see the looming problems in your personal life. You're just too consumed to pause and evaluate. It's only after looking back that you realize that the trade-off of money for the neglected relationships was never worth it. My family meant everything to me, but I didn't know enough then to realize that *providing* for my family was not as important as *being present* for my family.

Now fully conscious of that idea, I never wanted MOP or real estate to get in the way of me being present with my family again. My loved ones were a currency far more valuable than any precious metal or additional paycheck.

Being around family became exponentially easier as Jordan informed me that he was moving his crew back to Ohio. I hired him immediately at MOP. He still needed to learn a lot about the industry, but the thought of my only son one day taking over the family business was very inspiring to me. Now I could firmly see that MOP would continue to be a Yates legacy.

One of the unexpected benefits of Jordan's move was the magic of having my grandchildren nearby. I was determined to be a part of my kids' and grandkids' lives on a level that I had not yet experienced. The beauty of being a grandfather is acknowledging my shortcomings in the relationships with own children and getting a second chance to make them better. The grandchildren are a clean slate. Much like business failings, you assess what went wrong and then make a plan so that you don't repeat the issues. I knew I still had personal communication weaknesses (especially about showing my emotions), but I wanted to change for the better, no matter how much time and effort it took. Pursuing intentionality, my paradigm shifted to make my family more important than the business. I still made sure I was on top of things at MOP, but I scheduled as much time as I could with my kids and their children. I am so blessed to have amazing grandchildren. If you are open to them, children can teach you so much. My grandchildren have certainly unlocked the cheerful and playful side of my life that I didn't realize had been lying dormant inside me for so long.

Kids in general have this amazing ability to be free, happy, and full of love. Yet to be jaded by social media, negative influences, and the stressors of society, children haven't let the pressures of the world zap their power or dim their light. Ultimately, the real magic is to never lose that little kid inside. Hang on to that childlike faith and creativity that permeated your youth and refuse to embrace any part of hyper-self-awareness that holds you back as an adult.

With Jordan back in Ohio and on the MOP team, our father-son bond was improving rapidly. However, I was concerned that working together closer than ever had the potential to derail that relationship. I wanted him to be his own person and not feel like he was in my shadow, so I decided to place him in the transmission division where he could make his own name. Different from distribution, the transmission business involves connecting large pipe city-to-city and state-to-state.

Because I'd never been able to get this side of the business dialed in, there were numerous years when our company lost money on the transmission side. The bidding process and conditions in transmissions were some of the toughest in the industry. Even after securing the business, implementation could be quite challenging as it meant running pipe up and down steep terrain. It also happened to be the area where we had the most employee issues at MOP. In fact, this was the area that had played the largest part in torpedoing the Strike deal. To say the least, the transmission side was *messy*. However, it was this dysfunction that could forge Jordan into a serious leader. I prepared him that this would not be a walk in the park, but more akin to getting tossed out of an airplane at thirty thousand feet without a parachute and plummeting straight into a lion's den.

Jordan wasn't even given a title; he just jumped right in. Truthfully, I don't think a title mattered much to him as he was eager to analyze our business operations and learn the bidding process. Understandably, Jordan's sudden presence put certain employees on high alert as they knew he would see any indiscretions. Jordan immediately validated his unnamed position by picking up the business quickly. Using software to create algorithms, he swiftly figured out more effective ways to bid on projects.

For all of 2015, I focused on growing the distribution side of the business while Jordan was deeply ingrained in steering the transmission side to success. By the fall, his grasp of the business and innovative approach had won over both customers and employees. The cleanup process continued as Jordan and I began identifying the workers whom we had deemed as vampires to morale and the business. One by one, we examined each employee and found that most of the bad apples made our decision to fire them very easy. It turned out numerous people within the business needed to go.

Once we cleaned house, the dark cloud evaporated. It was a palpable change that everyone in the office could feel. I became inspired as I witnessed smiles and laughter returning to our shop and jobsites. Once I got rid of the negativity, I created room for positivity to come in.

This was still a relatively new concept for me at the time, but as we shed the dead weight, we had no choice but to go Up! When an area of your life is full of negativity, you have no room to add anything else to it. The minute you make space by getting rid of that negativity, God will fill it with something of far more value. In fact, it turns out positive people have an affinity for positive workplaces. Suddenly we found ourselves hiring fantastic new employees who added value and energy to the company.

It was obvious to me that Jordan's return to Ohio was not a coincidence. It was part of a greater plan that was playing out in front of me. I needed to keep my mind clear and balanced so I didn't miss any part of it. I couldn't help but look back and appreciate how all of this had started when I decided I was truly ready for change in my life in 2008.

As you've read throughout this book, every time I intentionally moved toward bettering myself, God showed up. It's not that He isn't always there; it's just that in the moments when we finally make ourselves available, we find him. I've heard it said that God's love is an infinite, roaring waterfall, and it's always flowing regardless of whether we believe in it or not. It is up to us to make the decision to step into the flow if we want to get wet. We have to be willing to move into the water to feel His presence. The inverse it true as well. We are free to stand on the sidelines and stay dry, but the waterfall will continue to thunder on without us.

The positivity that rippled through my organization unexpectedly began to fill up my personal life as well. Even though I wasn't looking, God must have thought I was finally ready to have someone special in my life.

Providence can be so sweet.

Chapter 11

THE SETUP

I wasn't looking for love. In fact, I was so focused on my family and the business that I didn't have time for a serious relationship. Then, of course, I met her. Her beauty first caught my eye, but something told me that her soul was the real treasure. I took a chance and asked her to go out for a drink.

Christina was divorced with three children. Just like me, she was knee-deep into her healing process. Her identity had been deeply rooted in "wife," and she needed the time to deconstruct her old programming and find her new inner self. Once we began talking and learning about each other, our paths felt so similar that it was eerie.

Her standards were tall—like Mount Everest tall—and she would prove be a tough catch. With the majority of her first dates, she had known within the initial ten minutes if that person was worth a second date. Even if you were lucky enough to get that second or third date, as soon as she realized you weren't *the one*, she ended it. She wasn't here to play games.

She kept a dating journal of all her experiences. The vast majority of the entries were odd or funny moments with commentary on each. Apparently, the note she wrote next to our first date was short and simple. In big red letters "MARRY HIM" was scribbled next to my name. She held that card close to her chest, and I only learned that helpful tidbit of information after we were married. To be honest, it was probably a good move as both Christina and I like a little bit of the chase.

Immediately, there was a level of comfort between us that neither of us had ever experienced with the opposite sex. It was as if we had known each other forever—as if we had grown up together. She is a force of nature who is passionate about life and teems with elegant energy. It didn't surprise me in the least to learn that she was a cancer survivor. Both of our healing processes included physical, mental, and spiritual components.

I was different from the other men whom Christina had met. I like to think my confidence and swagger fascinated her, but she insists she was actually attracted to my heart. Her spiritual eyes must have been wide open to see straight through my facade of bravado and deep into my heart.

We quickly became inseparable as I brought her into my world of concerts, parties, traveling, and driving fast. She was always down for my impulsive adventures, but what impressed me most about Christina was her love for others. We found our definition of fun shifting from things that entertained us to things that enriched our souls. It was evident that God's timing for our first encounter was precise. Had we met earlier in life, even after our divorces, neither one of us would have been ready to be a fruitful partner. We were both broken, and two damaged people don't make one healthy relationship. I don't care what Jerry Maguire says, you can't expect the other person to complete you. It takes two complete people to make one complete relationship work.

Incorporating Christina into my life became a treat. One of my favorite holiday things to do was go to the cancer ward at Columbus's Nationwide Children's Hospital and take gifts to the children. Ten years in a row, I would never call the hospital or get official clearance to do this. I would just slip in and walk the halls with a bundle of toys and gift cards to hand out to the parents and their sick children.

Obviously, playing secret Santa was very special to me. The parents were polite and grateful for the gifts, but they were also emotionally raw. For many of these families, each day that their child survives is a celebration. The slightest bit of good news from a negative test result is worth raucous praise and jubilation. When you are living your life at the extreme edges, you are numb to normal interactions. Meeting these families and their children was a somber perspective reset on my life. As I saw needles and tubes that had been inserted into these little children's bodies, my perceived problems suddenly, and rightfully so, became minor inconveniences.

The first time I brought Christina with me on my Secret Santa mission, we poked our heads into one of the rooms and saw a grandmother with her grandchild. The little girl sat in a bed tethered to an IV bag filled with neon-colored liquid. Her grandmother told us they had traveled from West Virginia to get special treatments for her granddaughter. In dire straits, they had spent the last of their money filling their gas tank to get them to the Children's Hospital. She tearfully admitted that they weren't even sure how they would get back home. She was just praying and trusting there would be a way. We happily handed her some gift cards and cash.

The grandmother began to shake.

Sobbing, she told us that we had to have been sent by God. Not only was she getting treatment for her granddaughter, but earlier that day her other grand-daughter had been killed in a car accident. She was wondering where God was in all of the chaos and destruction of the lives of her loved ones. If she couldn't be strong for her granddaughter getting the chemo, she was certain life wasn't worth living. I couldn't fathom the pain this woman was feeling, and I make no claims to understand how God allows such tragic things to happen in this world. That wasn't my question to answer, and even if I could, that's not what she needed in that moment. All she had been asking for was a sign to ease her mind and restore her faith. The fact that God could use Christina and I to comfort her for Him was a blessing to us as well. We are not saints, but we ministered to her as best we could.

I will always remember Nina too. I can't recall all the medical terms that were scrawled across her chart, but I learned that this nine-year-old did not let those words define her. As Christina and I continued to make our rounds, I turned a corner and saw her. Sitting in a hospital-issued wheelchair mid-hallway, Nina had a friendly smile and little-girl curls that were spilling over her face. In fact, one curl danced just in front of her eyepatch. I continued to walk toward her, trying to ignore the potent disinfectant smell plaguing the hallways. I grabbed a gift out of my bag and prepared to do the hand off.

Before I could greet her, she said in the cutest little voice, "How are you today, mister?" Her radiance melted me. As I knelt down beside her, I noticed the Jonas Brothers blanket draped across her wheelchair.

"You must be cold, huh?" She smiled and said, "It just makes me feel more normal to stay covered." I looked down and realized that there were no legs under her blanket. My tears started quickly, and I had no idea how to fully understand the emotions monopolizing my entire being. My heart broke for her, but I didn't want Nina to know it. I assumed that cancer had taken one of her eyes and probably both of her legs. I had to look away, but I didn't want Nina to think the sight of her repulsed me. I turned my head, took a breath, and wiped my face. She just put her hand and my shoulder and smiled an otherworldly smile. The only way I can try to describe it is that it was both comforting and sanctified. Then she asked me if I were OK. A little girl in the cancer ward with one eye and no legs genuinely wanted to make sure that I was OK. It rocked my world, and to this day, I still cannot fully describe that unique moment or that special human being.

I thought I was going to go bless her, but she blessed me. Until you go through being swept up in a moment like that, I don't know that you can fully comprehend it. That day I had received more than I ever thought I would. She touched a part of my soul that will be forever changed. It was like her hand, smile, and earnest words removed the last parts of negativity still hiding in the darkest places of my psyche. She purged me in a way that allowed more room in my heart for the right things.

There was pure magnetism radiating off Nina. God had equipped her with something that most of us don't have—the ability to impart serenity to those around her. Her body was wrecked, but she had a spirit that was like nothing I had ever known. She wasn't just sharing it with me; she was giving it to the world.

People come into our lives for a reason. The cast of valuable characters who have appeared throughout my life were never products of random happenstance. From professional mental coach to nine-year-old cancer patient, each encounter has prepared me to get ready for what was to come and not lose sight of myself along the way.

In 2013, I was traveling back and forth to Arizona and other locations for work. Being a bachelor (stereotypical as this may sound), I wanted someone to help keep up with my house in Westerville, Ohio. I put out a want ad, and Crystie entered my life. A pleasant woman with a generous smile who was then in her mid-sixties, her job was to check in on my property when I wasn't there and take care of basic household needs. She quickly became more than that as I grew to count on her as a personal assistant. Again, that was not in her original job description, but she didn't mind. The more time we spent together, the more I not only depended on her actions, but also on her wise counsel. The employee-boss relationship shifted as our friendship strengthened.

It has been said that everyone needs a Paul, Timothy, and Barnabas in their lives. We need a mentor, someone to mentor, and an encourager. I had my mentors and my protégés, and in Crystie I found my Barnabas. With a beautiful spirit and motherly advice, she invigorated me with kind words and a listening ear. When I felt lost, she would confirm to me that I was on the right path. With a loving heart, she had the ability to inspire me on the darker days when I felt unlovable. I didn't see it right away as she was my housesitter, but I can safely say that Crystie has been one of the top five most influential people in my life.

Each day, Crystie's heartfelt words and guidance energized me. Her practical and spiritual intuition were very powerful, and I trusted her judgment. She suggested we start a reading list. Every time I recommended a book to add, she was always way ahead of me having already read it and ingested its message. I soon realized the reading list was meant to be confirmation for me, rather than for Crystie's personal growth. With a voracious appetite for truth and compassion, she didn't need help finding her own peace. She was already there. A steadfast rock, Crystie's power was embedded in confidently knowing who she was and what she stood for as a person. Once you arrive at this spiritual plateau, you are able to be a mentor for others on their journey. In that strange sense, Crystie was not only my Barnabas, she also became my Paul.

In our conversations she had mentioned that she had battled cancer but had been free of the disease for many years. I never probed too deeply into the details about her illness because it was in her past and we were focused on the present. Several years into our friendship, I noticed the sparkle in her eyes dimming slightly with each visit. It was obvious that she was doing her best to put on a happy face for me, but something was chaining her down.

Once she could no longer hide it, she confided that the disease was back. Her news got worse as the doctors had told her that this time it was likely terminal. Suddenly my mind was racing as I recalled going through a similar horrific chemo scenario with my dad. Devastated, I prayed the treatment would work for her and that she wouldn't experience any crippling side effects.

Even though Crystie had started her exhausting chemo, she was determined to keep working for me as long as she could. I invited her to take it easy and focus on herself, but she wouldn't think of it. Sitting at home with nothing to do would have been more of a detriment to Crystie than cancer or chemotherapy.

After three months of torturous treatment, she came to me and said with as much dignity as she could, "You know, I can't go on. I've only got a couple of months to live, and I'm just tired." On that evening in my living room, Crystie had little desire to talk about the past or the present. She needed to discuss the future. The effects of the drugs were evident on her body, and she was certain she only had two months to live at best. However, she refused to leave me until she could find the appropriate replacement to take her place. That was a gut punch full of selfless dedication. With her life winding down, Crystie was still concerned with making sure someone was taking care of me. I wish I could have grasped her lesson of self-sacrifice at this time. No one could replace her. I knew my life would be very different with Crystie no longer in it.

Not wanting to disrupt the little time she had left with her family, I kept in touch with her through quick phone calls and texts for the next few months. One day,

I received a surprise message from Crystie inviting me to a party. It wasn't necessary to qualify it as a "goodbye party"; I already knew the gravity of the occasion. I offered to have the entire event catered, but that was not Crystie's style. She saw the beauty of having all of her friends and family bringing personal words and sentiments to share with the group.

I found myself strangely concerned about attending the party alone. Days before the event, the emotional impact of saying goodbye to this godly woman whom I loved really hit me. Without a friendly shoulder to lean on, I knew there was the possibility that I wouldn't make it through the night. I asked Christina if she'd accompany me.

As much as I was dreading attending, I was excited to see my friend again—even in her depleted state. During the drive to Crystie's house, I reflected upon our relationship and hoped our time together had been a blessing to her because I knew how much she had impacted me. As I parked the car, I prayed this whole shindig wouldn't feel grim and morose. I had never been to a "Goodbye Party." As Christina and I approached the house, I could hear the hum of numerous conversations and the sounds of laughter from her front yard. Instantly, I was at ease. *Fun and laughter?* Of course, Crystie would be celebrating life and not mourning its inevitable conclusion. She would have had it no other way!

Inside, I found Crystie sitting on her couch. The chemo had not been kind to her body. She was bald and frail with emaciated shoulders that drooped under the strain of her failing condition. Surrounded by a throng of friends and family, I didn't want to be rude and interrupt her conversation.

Christina and I made the rounds through the house as we waited for an opening to say hello to Crystie. When the timing was right, we found a spot next to her on the couch. There was so much I wanted to tell her, but I simply couldn't find the right words. I was allowing my brain instead of my heart to dictate the conversation. Unfortunately, the mind filters so much of what the heart yearns to speak.

Plus, what do you say to someone who will pass soon?

Unsurprisingly, through our conversation I learned that Crystie's spirit was even more full and bright than I'd remembered. Her strength confounded me. Her gratitude was unparalleled. Here was a woman who had every reason to be angry with God because her days were numbered, but instead she was grateful for all the days she had been given. Even in this final visit, Crystie was still teaching me. Unbelievable.

When we got up to leave, Crystie grabbed my arm with a tender strength that surprised me. I thought she might need my help to rise, but before I could pull her up, she looked me right in the eyes and said, "You were my purpose."

I definitely didn't know what to say or really what she meant, to be honest. It's such a grand statement in such a delicate moment. Again, here was a second chance to pour out my heart to her, but I just smiled and nodded. I stepped away without any additional words so someone else could be near her on the couch.

At times, I don't pick up on things like I should. Truthfully, it took the dedicated work of all my mentors in Phoenix to open my eyes to this fact as they pulled me out of my physical, mental, and spiritual funk. I stood perplexed in the kitchen as I replayed Crystie's final words in my mind.

Thankfully, a woman approached me and introduced herself as one of Crystie's closest friends. By her thoughtful demeanor I could tell we were not about to embark upon a surface conversation of pleasantries and commentary on the weather. We carved out a corner of the kitchen for a more private experience as she confided, "You mean so much to Crystie. She has lived longer because she wanted to take care of you. You really are her purpose."

There was something transcendent about hearing the word *purpose* twice that made everything suddenly fall into place. I knew how much Crystie had impacted my life, but I had no idea how much I had played a role in hers until that moment. The crazy part was that what I was doing for her had nothing to do with me; she didn't need much from me. I was her purpose because she believed in me when I didn't believe in myself. She saw a bright future for me while I was busy being stuck in my troubled past. That was enough for Crystie. I suddenly felt honored and guilty in the same breath.

A couple of weeks after the party, Crystie went home to be with Jesus. And I had a responsibility to live up to her expectations of me.

As I look back, I am so grateful for all of her sage advice and guidance. She had covered me with wisdom that had impacted me immediately and counsel that had filled my subconscious and would not emerge until later in my life. Her passing made me cognizant of how the Old Me operated in relationships—only interested in getting what I desired from people without considering their needs. It may sound harsh, but my mind was in "go mode" at all times, and I moved at a speed that didn't allow me to slow down to pay attention to others. Thankfully, this is not the case anymore.

Chapter 12

THE REBUILD

*E*verything in my life felt like it was continually moving Up, and I could feel that 2016 was the start of something special. Jordan and I were excelling at rebuilding our business, but more importantly, our relationship. Like any good father, I'm sure I frustrated him at times, but I couldn't make it too easy on him. There's no fun in that.

The boy had my DNA and that of my father before me, so I wanted to impart my learned philosophy of balance between work and life. Don't get me wrong; I was also very busy at MOP during that time, but I made certain I didn't get lost in it all. I tried to make sure Jordan didn't either as he was straining to manage his roles of husband and father with being the heir apparent of MOP. I prayed that he was not following in my old footsteps, but rather in my new ones. However, he is a Yates, so I knew the best plan was to never approach the situation directly. Instead, I would keep walking the walk around him and let time tell if my strategy had worked. I had to trust God that day by day or maybe even month by month, my son would be open to a different and healthy mindset.

Financially, MOP had needed to start over. Our valuation and fiscal condition had fallen sharply since the ruined sales offer with Strike in 2014. None of this fazed me much because I was too busy living life gratefully. I made a decision to wake up every day, do my exercises, and choose gratefulness. Starting your morning with positive energy and gratitude have the ability to pull you through the day. This takes practice and proactiveness. No matter the circumstance, focus on the things that you can be thankful for. I could be grateful to have my health, my family, and my company (even if it wasn't as valuable as it once was).

With my mind, body, and soul stronger than ever, I decided it was time to accelerate the company Up, even if it meant taking some risks. Here's the crazy part—it wasn't about my ego. Finally after all these years, I could safely say that ego was no longer driving my desire to make more money and have the biggest, baddest company in the industry. I wanted to make more to save more to—you know where this is headed—give more!

The greatest things you can do in life are things that you can't achieve on your own. For so long, I felt like Atlas trying to hold the entire weight of MOP on my shoulders. I had slowly pared away responsibilities, and it had cost me. It wasn't until Jordan came on board that I was truly comfortable counting on someone else to handle many of the intricacies of the business. It could have been the familial ties and trust factor, or it could have been that he was so dang good at his job! Jordan had a vision on avenues to streamline systems and processes across the board. It was his gift; definitely not mine. He crafted a standardized bidding process that made it easy for anyone inside the company to implement and replicate. I had been too comfortable relying on the processes that had worked in the past, but Jordan recognized all the holes that were sinking our ship in the current industry environment.

Allowing my son to focus on the nuts and bolts enabled me to shift my focus to the people. I found my leadership style evolving. The natural progression of my personal healing allowed me the confidence to open up to my employees on a more personal level. In conversations, I was receiving and no longer only dictating. I became obsessed with team morale and evaluating ways to improve it. With empathy, I sought out employees who were struggling and shared how my mindset shift had begun my healing process. My testimony was clear proof that mental, physical, and spiritual workouts can change your life. Surprisingly, I found myself less concerned about the bottom line dollars at MOP and more passionate about guiding the teams to think about life differently.

This may not sound like much, but these were blue-collar construction workers smack-dab in the Midwest. The topics of our talks were not typical boss-employee conversations around these parts, and it was a mystery to me if they were just appeasing me because I was the owner or because my words were really making a difference. But as time went on, those conversations became longer and deeper. It was a delightful dance as the more receptive my employees became to my lifestyle conversations, the more comfortable I felt sharing my advice and the deeper parts of my journey. Guards came down and there was a snowball effect that tangibly rumbled through our workforce.

An avalanche of gratitude.

Have you ever heard a song in which the lyrics were so true that you had to pull over or stop what you were doing to just listen? I felt that way the first time I heard Tim McGraw's song "Humble and Kind."

Hold the door, say please, say thank you
Don't steal, don't cheat, and don't lie
I know you got mountains to climb
But always stay humble and kind
When those dreams you're
dreamin' come to you
When the work you put in is realized
Let yourself feel the pride
But always stay humble and kind.[4]

This became my theme song for 2016. I couldn't get the words out of my head and found myself listening to the song over and over on repeat. I wanted to share its message, so I would send it to friends and family. "Humble and Kind" is one of those rare songs that transcends anything lyrically and actually feels like it becomes a part of your DNA. I realize that sounds extreme, but with the talk of mountains and pride, Tim was speaking directly to my soul.

Even if I tried to convince myself that I was totally selfless, I knew I still had an ego as I sparred with my negative character traits daily. Countering humanness is constant work, especially when you are sitting atop a company with five hundred employees. Although I was letting go of any harshness in my leadership communication style, I was still a work in progress. Constantly learning and improving, I truly desired to create a welcoming atmosphere at MOP where all of my employees felt safe, seen, heard, and valued.

Great leaders are always walking a tightrope without a net. It is a delicate balance to get it right as workers want to see that you're grateful, but you also better have the ability to unblinkingly rally your troops and say, "We are going up that hill right there, you are coming with me, and here's why." There is an inherent powder-keg authority built into leadership that has to be contained to avoid repulsing people. However, at the same time, you must display complete confidence and a clear vision so that those you are leading are motivated to follow you.

I wanted to cement the theme of Tim McGraw's song into our corporate culture at MOP. I needed a platform to speak from my heart and inspire our company from a place of humility and love. My workforce needed to truly understand top-down leadership, and this song summarized everything that I, as a person, wanted to be as well as all that MOP should encompass.

At our Christmas party, I played the music video on a big screen before I took the stage. As the video played, I watched the faces of my employees. You could read the room, as one by one the impact was made evident. Once the video stopped, I could have taken the stage to give an epic speech full of extravagant promises and stirring action points, but I didn't have to do any of that. I let the powerful message of the song speak for me. The lyrics embraced everything I wanted to share with my five hundred employees and their spouses. My speech was short and succinct. Gone were the litany of numbers and industry jargon from Christmas speeches of the past. Instead, I spoke out of love and compassion to supplement the lyrics of the song. When we resumed work at MOP after the Christmas vacation, the attitudes cascading from my highest-level employees down to the interns shuffling coffee and papers were visibly different. This was a demonstrable turning point both for the company and me, and it was all birthed from a song.

> *Don't take for granted the*
> *love this life gives you*
> *When you get where you're going*
> *Don't forget turn back around*
> *And help the next one in line*
> *Always stay humble and kind.*[5]

While there have been several books written on the subject (irony alert: you're currently reading one), to me gratitude isn't simply a theoretical way of thinking. *Gratitude* is a verb. It is an active way to live your life that deeply and profoundly alters the ways you think and feel. Maybe everything isn't going as planned in your life and it feels too daunting or hypocritical to be grateful for health (you're sick), money (it's hard to pay bills), or family (they seem more like foes). That's understandable; start small. Find something (anything) you can be grateful for, even if it's thanking God for the air you breathe. Trust me, it all matters. Those other circumstances will change, but don't live your life ungratefully until they do. You will be miserable. My secret to going Up is the more gratefulness I feed my mind, the more abundant my life becomes.

Christina's and my dating journey was a push-pull struggle between my head and my heart. In the beginning, I was just having fun and was not interested in anything too serious. Marriage had failed me once before and I was afraid of what the past could mean for my future. Plus, I didn't want anything or anyone tying me down or holding me back. However, as we grew closer, my heart was working hard to convince my brain to push past all the roadblocks because she was *the one.*

Turns out that my heart was on to something as Christina is perfect for me in so many ways. I am a better man because of her, and I had never been in a relationship like that before. With an exuberant passion for life, she is a constant giver to the people around her. She is smart and savvy, yet her feet are firmly planted on the ground. It also doesn't hurt that she is so staggeringly sexy!

Even though she was my ideal woman, I struggled to be all-in. No longer afraid to work out the perplexing thoughts in my head, I continued to identify the things that were holding me back in regard to "us." I knew I needed some extra help for my heart to convince my head, so I spoke regularly with my mentors back in Arizona and continued to do the hard work on myself. I was afraid that if I weren't able to overcome my past shortcomings, fear would shut me down and I could sabotage this relationship.

Love is a funny thing. Good things come into our lives when we learn to accept love and understand that we're worthy of love. We think we understand the concept, and then something happens that amplifies our definition of love. Before I went to Crystie's party or visited the Children's Hospital, I thought I understood how to receive love. I couldn't have been more wrong. Having people pour into my healing made me realize that I was worthy of love. Really, the bedrock for any love is the unconditional kind. God is the ultimate teacher of that *agape*—love we can't earn; it's just selflessly given. Once we receive that unbridled, unmerited love, our armor falls off and we allow all types of love to enter into our being.

Focusing on the positive allowed me to eventually see that my desire for the woman who loved me trumped my fears that I wouldn't be able to effectively love her back. I had been growing for me, but now I needed to grow for her. I was terrified, but by Christmas 2016, I had a ring and a plan. The location of the proposal was a no-brainer. I wanted to get her not only back to Phoenix, but also to the mountain that had saved my life. She was the ultimate step in a process that began at the top of Camelback.

Now, I know you don't know Christina, but I can assure you that she was going to make me earn it. I've closed numerous transactions with some very seasoned dealmakers, but talking her into going to Phoenix so close to the holidays while her kids were at home was possibly the toughest negotiation of my career. She is an amazing mother and wanted to be home with them. I'm still not sure if I convinced her to go, or if it were something in her soul, but somehow I got her there!

The whole time we were in Phoenix, the energy between us felt different. I was nervous and distant as I struggled to be present with her. My mind was playing out five hundred scenarios in a loop in my mind of how the proposal was going to go at the end of the week. Furthermore, Christina had no idea that I had picked out a ring two months prior and was waiting for it to come in the mail! If that ring didn't make it to the hotel in time, there would be no proposal. Needless to say, things were not going as planned.

However, Christina didn't know my psychological backstory for the trip, and my unusual behavior wasn't going over well. She had sacrificed to come on this vacation, and she wanted me all-in. A couple of days into the trip, the volatile mixture of being away from her kids and my awkward behavior created the perfect storm for some solid Christina homesickness. She woke up in the middle of the night and got on her phone to check out flights on Priceline. Thankfully, I opened an eye as she was booking a flight back to Ohio the next afternoon. This was a huge problem. Since the ring still had not arrived, everything was planned and prepared for me to propose on the last day of the trip!

Full of legitimate anxiety, I implored her to stay just one more day with me in Phoenix. I knew it would be best for both of us if I moved up my proposal time frame to, like, immediately! However, my strategy was to play small ball and each day convince her to stay one more day. It would take a monumental amount of persuasion, but until that ring arrived, I was stuck.

God has a funny way of working things out; the ring arrived the next morning. Since I no longer needed to dissuade Christina from leaving, it was time to put the plan into action.

The entire time we had been dating, I continually spoke to her about how critical Camelback Mountain had been to my recovery. If she had met the man I was before I conquered that mountain, we wouldn't be where we were then—or now. That Old Brent would have never been able to function inside a healthy relationship. In that way, this mountain meant so much to *us*. We could see those foothills rising to the peak from our hotel, but I still had not taken her there. Yet. We were set to climb Camelback Mountain in the afternoon, and then she could go home to be with her kids.

As we walked up the mountain, all the feels came back, and I just couldn't contain myself. I had run this mountain so many times in my renewal process that it felt wrong to just walk it. As I broke out into a jog, I eyed Christina behind me. I could tell that she was a little irked, but being a stud athlete, she picked up her pace as well. To reassure her this was not going to be a full-blown sprint to the top, I called back to her, "There's a little area behind the mountain halfway up. I want to show you the city."

I led her along the pathway leading to my favorite overlook. On any normal day, I would gaze down at the beautiful architecture of the numerous buildings below juxtaposed and cradled by the natural splendor of God's mountains. But on this day, I saw my future bride silhouetted against the endless valley. Nearly out of breath, I grabbed her shoulders and turned her outward to take in the majestic view.

"This is it."

After all of my bragging about Camelback, my almost bride-to-be was logically under the assumption that I was referencing the dazzling outlook. She stood and silently scoped the powerful mountains and city brimming with life nestled inside of it. At that moment, I got down on my knee and waited for her to turn back around. Finally, she did—

"Will you marry me?"

It was as if I hammered a stake in the ground right there in that city, on that mountain, that vista with the woman whom I love to claim that I have arrived. Everything finally came together for me in that moment. For the first time, my past felt just like that—*the past*. I was totally in the present and emotionally available, but the best part was that I could finally, decisively see the future.

Chapter 13

A STRANGE TIME TO LET GO

*T*he New Year was shaping up to be unbeatable! Everything in my life was lining up for success, both personally and professionally. I was engaged to the woman of my dreams, my employees and family loved me, and business had picked back up. In fact, it was almost going too well. Here's the crazy part: I couldn't seem to find my joy.

You see, I had set my bar so low that I believed contentment was all I deserved. That was a lie. That was the devil on my shoulder. With my life really taking shape, my mind was subconsciously looking for the next bad thing to happen. It was an impending relapse of negativity because I just couldn't accept that I was in a really healthy place in my life. I fought it the best I could by practicing staying positive and countering the old garbage thoughts with new, constructive reflections.

You have the capacity to govern what you think. Oftentimes when you are mired in the negative, you can refocus your mind to a new subject or mindset. Many times it involves finding peace and relying on God to help solve the problem. You will have to choose to trust God and, in turn, trust yourself. Put on the armor of God because when you protect your mind and heart, you safeguard your balance.

Furthermore, if I weren't acutely controlling my thoughts, I found I would slip back into looking for an opponent to battle. Most times, these unsuspecting people had no idea that I had pegged them as my rivals. Whether it was innate or the athlete in me always looking for a challenger, I still had a warrior's mentality of looking to conquer. Focusing on my holistic exercises and training, I was constantly unwinding my old train of thought and replacing it with the understanding that life works with me, not against me. I would think back to all the past examples of how I had been lovingly supported on my path (sometimes by the most unlikely people). I trusted the process and flow of life with my new mindset.

An important component of my morning visualization practice was mentally reviewing how I had responded to specific situations the day before. If I paid close attention, I could track how certain emotional and mental patterns showed up in my personal and business lives. Some days I crushed it at living in the new construct, and other days my humanness and ego choked me out. Even on those off days, I refused to live in regret as that would have been entrenched in shame and guilt. Instead, I took the time to be grateful for my present and energized about my future. Eventually, I was able to accept happiness above contentment.

Christina and I set a date for the wedding and plans were underway. The business was expanding and growing better every day, and I had not lost sight of spending time on myself or with Jordan and my family. I was flourishing as a father and really stepping into my role as "Pa," which is what my grandchildren call me.

While I was at peace, I was never complacent. I was living life with zeal, and if all my buckets felt full, it just meant it was time to find more buckets! On the business side, MOP was more valuable than ever, and I cared deeply, sympathetically about my people and my family's legacy.

That is exactly why I was ready to sell the company.

Now, that may sound strange considering what I just said, but we had created a culture and a certain way of life at MOP, and I knew my people would be OK even if I were no longer in charge. I was weary after all these years of being captain, and I had set the ship on a course ready to sail on its own. That's the legacy part. By now, Jordan was an irreplaceable cog in our machine and excelled at running the show. If we sold, I was confident the buyers would take care of my son and keep him in his leadership position.

Remembering the unnerving sale process in 2014 and how it had affected me, I made sure my decision wasn't rash. I prayed, meditated, and felt that it was time for me to move on to bigger things.

Bigger than a company of five hundred people? Absolutely.

If we sold the company, my mantra of "make more, save more, give more" would have the ability to elevate to a much higher level. Shifting my focus from the day-to-day operations of the company would free me to concentrate on spreading positivity to a much bigger sphere of influence. I saw visions of myself helping to shift the world culture into being more "humble and kind."

So in the summer of 2017, I officially decided to sell my beloved MOP. This time I was going to own the experience and not allow it to get bigger than me. I put everything in motion and hired another broker to manage the process. It was going to take at least four to six months to get MOP back on the market, so I let the broker do all the preliminary work to get us going. Besides, I had something much bigger on the horizon: my wedding.

It is amazing to witness the power of being in alignment with yourself. That doesn't happen by accident; it is a conscious decision to honor your mind, body, and spirit. More accurately, it is a constant daily continuum of honoring. For me, that started the day I decided to no longer sacrifice my health, routine, or faith just to serve my ego. The place I find myself now in my life is the culmination of all the hard work I've put in over the past ten years. And that I continue to put in. Once you find yourself in a place of balance, you are ready to give your greatest self to the world.

Balance provides clarity. I accepted the equation that I had to make more (receive), save more (own it for myself), and be able to give more (share myself with the world). When you think about it, you can't give someone water from an empty cup. You first must receive water into your own cup if you want to share it with others. You also can't give it all away because you will go thirsty in the process.

I found that my happiness was not rooted in the money I made but in the peace of giving it away to better the world. In that way, it became a cyclical pattern in which the more I gave financially, the more I received spiritually. It became a perpetual cycle with the reward being an abundant and flowing life.

On June 17, 2017, I was fully prepared to receive the biggest blessing of my life—my wife. During the wedding planning there had been dozens of little synchronicities and coincidences that validated our decision to get married. It started with Jorgensen Farms, the venue that my daughter Lauren found. A perfect and coveted wedding location, it was booked a year in advance. Knowing the odds were against our date being available on such short notice, Christina still called to inquire. Much to her shock, Jorgensen Farms happened to have had a rare cancellation the day before, and the lone date that had been freed was the very day my bride-to-be was calling about—June 17. Even the wedding planner couldn't believe the odds. By this time, we had learned not to believe in chance. Instead, we believed in confirmation. The "coincidences" didn't stop there, as the specific caterer and DJ we wanted each had cancellations pop up for our June 17 weekend. It only made sense that friends and family who had previously told us they couldn't make it because of schedule conflicts suddenly found their calendars would be free as well.

Not only was God's divine hand helping us out, He was making it really obvious. Trust me when I confide that I needed all the help I could get. I didn't let on that I was suddenly hesitant about the whole thing. I was certain that I wanted to spend the rest of my life with Christina, but the remaining parts of my ego were keeping me imprisoned with dread. The signposts were unmistakably showing us that we were traveling the right road. My heart was already sold, but my brain needed a knockout punch to completely surrender.

The wedding rings were delivered.

Separately, we had gone to different jewelers to size our rings. There was never a conversation between us about getting anything engraved on our bands, but while at the shop, each of us decided to do it out of our own volition. When we presented each other with the rings, it was no surprise that we had both gotten the same three words etched inside our rings.

This is it.

Boom. While I definitely needed the push from God at the time, I didn't realize Christina did too. She was intuitive and could sense my mind wavering at times. Years later, she confessed that on our wedding day, she had given me a fifty-fifty chance of even showing up. I had no idea how much my trepidation had been surfacing right in front of her face. Thankfully, she trusted my heart over my head.

After what felt like an eternity of being alone, I'd finally found my soul mate. On that perfect summer day in June, I got married to the one woman on earth who is strong enough to stand beside me for a lifetime. With a pure heart and strength of character, she inspires me to be the best version of myself. I continually choose her every day, not just on our wedding day.

At the end of the day, if you truly want to be transformed, it comes down to one person—you. No one else can breathe for you; no one else can exist for you. It is and always will be up to you to choose your life. For me, that meant no longer blaming others and taking responsibility for my misfortunes. Finding yourself is key, as there is no moving Up if you are carrying the weight of everyone else, their expectations, and their dreams on your back.

That didn't mean I wasn't intended to be a leader or that I should stop caring about others. Conversely, once

I freed myself, I had the ability to lead from a much healthier, bigger place. If I really cherished people, I had to believe in them enough to empower them on their own path. Every person in the company was responsible for their own journey. It didn't matter if it were the person in the neon vest holding the caution sign on the street or my right-hand man, Jordan. I couldn't just be in the business of answers; I had to be the source for guidance.

That takes a different kind of thinking. It seems easier in the short term to tell people what to do, but they will end up relying on you instead of their own strength. So if you are really going to invest in your future and in your company's future, take the extra time to help others develop critical thinking skills in order to make decisions for themselves. Make a concentrated effort to teach instead of tell.

This same instructive mindset applies just as well to parents. As much as we try, we cannot possibly protect our children from "the world." So instead of shielding them, we have to empower them by reminding them daily that they are responsible for their own happiness, joy, and love. Relying on friends, sports, social media, or even their parents to be their source will only leave them feeling hollow. It begins with God and themselves. From there, you can be the loving, gentle hand that ushers them along the path.

My grandkids helped me realize that children start out being their own source of happiness and love. They are alive, full of life, and feisty. They don't see the barriers that we do because they aren't conditioned to operate out of fear as we are as adults. They really don't let much of anything stop them.

When my kids were young, I knew nothing about empowerment or the power of choice. In fact, my insistence to dictate their choices created a path of pain and struggle that carried over into their adulthood. I was programming my son and daughters the same way my parents unintentionally had programmed me. When Jordan came to MOP, I was fortunate to realize the error of my ways. Since I was in a healthier place, I recognized the need to step aside and empower him. Instead of focusing on what he should or shouldn't do, I concentrated on imparting the message that he was valued and respected. It was not just in the business sphere; it was a fatherly message that I needed my daughters to hear as well. No matter how my parenting was communicated, my children needed to know that my love for them was unconditional and there was nothing they could do to make me love them any more or any less. That was a difficult lesson I didn't learn until I finally viewed myself through the same lens through which God sees me. I trust that my children all know the way I feel now, but I will always strive to get better at saying it.

I put all of this aforementioned parental advice into motion when I asked Jordan to stand side by side with me through the sale of our family's company.

Typically, selling a company is a buyer's game as they are able to drive most of the terms and negotiations. It's their money, so this is to be expected. From the onset, I realized that that our sale would be different. We weren't coming from a place of weakness as we had been in the potential Strike sale. There was no "hoping" that someone would see the value in us. We were confident we would be in control. This was a huge moment for me. I understood this was my company to sell, but this time it was without the ego of thinking small and feeling overwhelmed. Also, there was no ego or cockiness. Just simple trust, truth, and faith. We knew who we were and what we were worth, and the right company would see that.

Once we listed the company for sale, it was a waiting game to see who was interested. The last time we had been on the market, we had fourteen prospective buyers approach us. We were an exponentially stronger company now, so we opened the floodgates in anticipation of being inundated with inquiries. And boy, did they come. Well, *one* came.

That was it. Out of the countless companies in our industry, only one had any interest in MOP. I was surprised and concerned, to say the least. There isn't much of a negotiation process if there is only one company at table. Also, with all of the due diligence and discovery process in front of us, the odds of closing a deal with only one company as an option was extremely small.

But then I remembered: you only need one.

The bidder was APi Group from Minnesota. The conglomeration services customers worldwide and owns more than forty-five different companies that have more than two hundred separate locations. APi Group owns companies in industries that range from safety, fire suppression, and steel fabrication, to energy and construction. The publicly traded company has a market cap of $3.49 billion,[6] which meant there were financial opportunities for everyone at MOP.

Truthfully, APi would have zero idea of how many companies were interested in us, whether it was one hundred or one. I was resolute that if APi were the right one, it wouldn't matter how many buyers were beating our doors down. Everything had been coming into alignment this whole time, and I had to trust this situation was no different. I went to work as the margin for error was nonexistent. Any sign hinting at a lack of confidence on our part could send this transaction spiraling down to the boneyard next to the old Strike debacle.

This was my deal to own, but doubt crept into my psyche. I was suddenly hampered by thoughts of failure and began questioning if I even had the ability to navigate the process now that our company had grown so large. After all, APi had negotiated countless deals of this nature before, and my only experience had ended in futility. This is where training comes into play.

I did some breath work and specific visualizations that recentered my negative thoughts and worry and reminded me that this was my deal to make, not theirs. APi may have purchased a multitude of companies, but they had never seen one like mine. We had no debt, great profitability, and we didn't need the sale or the money to be successful. We were in control.

Jordan and I started digging into APi's offer as soon as we got the details. Even on our initial examination, something felt different. They were in the business of purchasing smaller companies and letting them continue to operate in that mom-and-pop manner. I pored over their website to dive into their company from a cultural perspective. They talked about being one company; in fact, the number *one* was all over their website. As I read their mission statement, I was mesmerized that it coincided almost identically with my own company's core values of hard work, integrity, and great partnerships. Despite the size difference, it was evident that the philosophies of MOP and APi were solidly aligned.

Their LOI came quickly, and we accepted it. We started the dreaded due diligence process and initial meetings soon after. It was equal parts nerve-racking and exciting, but I loved the pace at which we were moving. I asked a catalog of questions about their company culture and the way they did business. MOP was my baby, and I wouldn't let it go to any company that I didn't love. I was interviewing them just as much, if not more, than they were interviewing me.

Jordan stepped into his role like an industry veteran. We were a robust team as neither tried to get ahead of the other. Our two egos were at ease and in check. During the negotiations I highlighted my son and his impact as much as I could. Unsurprisingly, when they quizzed him, he had all the right answers. I straight-out told APi that they were buying him as the future, not me. I would remain on the board, but I most definitely would not be running any day-to-day operations. Jordan knew that I would always be there for him, but my involvement in the company was secondary to the next chapter in my life that would begin when the sale closed.

Like Strike before them, API's auditors dug into our books, systems, and processes. They scoured for inefficiencies and discrepancies, and examined how we broke down profitability. Basically, they searched for anything they could find that would give the company an opportunity to discount its offer.

Remember how I said no regrets, only lessons? I didn't regret that we'd lost the Strike contract, but I took those lessons to prepare my company for the next time we found ourselves with a similar opportunity. Here we were again, except this time the auditors couldn't find anything major when they scrutinized us. Jordan and I had done such a great job correcting all our weaknesses that we were unyieldingly solid from top to bottom. Not only did I know it, but *they* knew it. There was still a road to travel, but recognizing that the fixes we'd made had paid off already felt like a victory.

Before they started real negotiations, I sat down with their board and said very clearly, "Based on our interactions and, culturally, the two companies both operating with a focus of being number one, you know we both offer each other extreme value. I wholeheartedly believe that we are supposed to be partners going forward. The original number you offered us is *the* number, and we absolutely bring that value. We are not going any further into the due diligence process or taking any less for our company. Know that we will deliver on everything we've said; if we can finish at this number, we have a deal. Your offer was not a starting point number; it is the final number."

I was clear and distinct. I knew who I was, and all my mistakes and victories had prepared me for this very moment. I was operating mindfully and intentionally. I wasn't trying to control this for the sake of ego or influence. I was betting on myself, my son, and this company. MOP was no longer just a family company, but an actual extension of my family. I knew that I was the best person to get us across that finish line. After the botched Strike deal, this was redemption.

And in February 2018, three months after the aforementioned conversation, the sale to APi was finalized. All in all, the purchase price of MOP was not important; the process is what is worth noting. I didn't forget the paths that led me there or the people who helped. I was grateful, and I preached an atmosphere of gratitude at MOP. There was nothing contractual required, but I gifted every employee with money from the sale. It didn't matter if the employee had been there a decade, a year, or a day. Without their hard work and commitment, MOP was worthless. In essence, we'd built this company together as team, and that was a huge mindset shift from the Old Brent. In fact, I believe the Lord held out on our first sale because I didn't have the proper mindset with regard to what it meant to selflessly share. I know if we had made the sale to Strike, I would have kept all the proceeds for myself. This day was different, and by lunchtime I had handed out over three million dollars to very grateful (and unsuspecting) workers. It was one of the best experiences of my life, and like every other time, the more I gave, the more I received.

We ended up being one of APi's best-performing companies in 2019 and 2020. That first year with Jordan as president of MOP, we performed at our highest net margin ever. Thanks to my son and other tireless MOP employees, my promise to APi that we would deliver was and still is being fulfilled.

To see the photos of Brent's real life journey and find free resources to begin your own life-changing journey, we invite you to visit here:

To check out the exclusive Gravity UPGear, please visit here:

Chapter 14

HEADING UP!

*I*t has been more than three years since the sale of the company, and I have continued to work on myself daily. The process of writing this book has been emotionally challenging for me as I have never publicly put myself out there. To be honest, it's taken this long for me to even be comfortable enough to see the value in sharing my story. As you have read, I was terrified of my company's audit, and these pages have essentially been a personal lifetime audit. My choices, mistakes, and missteps have been laid bare for others to see and examine. The beauty is that I learned how to move Up. I truly felt called by God to write this book so that others might be encouraged and feel the pull to come along with me. I'm no writer, but I pushed through any fear and chose to do this as an opportunity to give to the world and help others who are battling their Old Self while searching for a way to go Up.

I remember hesitantly telling Jordan that I was going to write a book, and he said, "You evolved when you did not have to. You could just be sitting on a beach enjoying your fat payday and a margarita, but you choose to be engaged and help others. I tell your stories all the time." I felt both surprise and confirmation. I never knew my son told my stories to anyone.

Honestly, he is right. I am fortunate enough that I never have to work another day in my life. I'm in a place where I own all my time, but I've learned that I'm eager to give it away to others. This book has been cathartic in many ways as I've thought about the moments and people that led me to where I am today. It has only strengthened my mind, body, and soul practice.

Furthermore, these pages are a public declaration that will keep me walking the walk.

The question is: what will this book help you do? With information comes choice. You now get to decide if you take this material and do something with it. If you choose to take no action, this will just be another book you read and your tomorrow will look just like your yesterday. I don't believe that's what you are after, though.

I want you to let this book be a part of the receiving side of your life. It is not just the information here; it is everything on our website (www.bethelead.me), the visualizations, the podcasts where I interview inspirational people, and the fun social media. I'm not trying to make money on this book; I don't need it. I've moved past the "make more, save more" portion of my life. I'm elated to be actively participating in the "give more" segment.

Another way I have created an opportunity to *give more* is with a self-funded charity Christina and I started in 2018. The charity is called RestoreUS (restoreus.com). With a unique model of giving, Restore US sees a need and rushes to meet that need. No red tape. No paperwork. Feet on the ground. Arms wide open. Radical generosity in action. When we go out in the name of radical giving—giving of our time, of our hearts, and of our resources—we, too, are restored.

If you are in need, we encourage you to go to our Restore Us website and tell us your story. While we can't help everyone, we certainly try to do our best. At the very least, we will pray for you and point you in the right direction of someone else who may be able to help.

I still manage my work-life balance pretty well. I have not stopped working, but it looks much different now. I spend much of my time teaming with business partners to build multi-family apartment developments in Arizona and Ohio. I call it "work," but it all flows pretty well. My ego of force and control still wants to come out at times, but I understand that energy doesn't serve me.

We are all searching for something more in life. I want you to know that the "more" you are searching for is *you*. Don't let anything or anyone be your answer because it is only up to you. Please know wherever you are on your journey, you are exactly where you need to be. Whether this is your first step forward to growth or your one millionth, if you take it all one step at a time, great things can happen. I have experienced it and watched it play out in others' lives time and time again. Be prepared that your humanness and ego will always be there to counter you along the way, but remember to listen to that angel on your shoulder. Do that, and the devil will flee! I assure you that there is always a way Up, no matter how hard the situation may be.

Never be discouraged when you think you've climbed the highest mountain in the range only to see a higher peak off in the distance. Growth is not about reaching one height and stagnating for the rest of your life. Growth is about accepting who you are today and knowing there is room in your life to climb that next summit. So don't stop now. Stay inspired to keep pushing, because there is really no limit to what you can achieve when you dream big and stay positive.

Stay all-in, remember that no one can hold you down, and be the lead of your own life.

Keep going Up!

ACKNOWLEDGMENTS

*F*irst and foremost, I need to thank GOD. I was his hardheaded Humpty Dumpty. Ignoring that vital spiritual relationship, I was continually falling and trying to put myself back together again with zero success. Except in my story, all the king's men (and women) who He did send my way were thankfully there to put me back together. He definitely put the right mentors and friends into my path to save my life. Without the Lord and His grace, I would still be lying broken after all those great falls.

To Christina, my rock. You encouraged me to write this book in 2016 when I was too scared to be exposed. I was fearful that my past could in some way shame my future. But you are my future, and you put that confidence and love inside of me that allowed me to finally share my story to help others move Up. I love you.

Krista and Lauren, my beautiful and understanding daughters. Our relationships have not been without ups and downs, but through those challenges have come the blessings! I know there was some understandable trepidation along the way as I shared my life and the journey of our family, but you confirmed me. You continue to confirm me to this day, and I draw strength from that. Thank you for your mercy and your love.

Through this soul-searching adventure, I've been able to explore the very important father-son relationship. My father was my mentor, and he loved holding that position. While I should have been grateful at the time, I did not respect the process until I became healthy. Dad, I am eternally grateful now.

A message to all sons—do not put self-imposed pressure on yourselves to be greater than your old man. Know that your father is pulling you up and you should be driving toward him. Move together, respect his position, and he will see you!

Jordan, my son, I have done my best to mentor you in a healthy way. I've always wanted to show you the ropes of the business, but now, more so than ever, I want to be there to show you the ropes of life. You are an amazing father, husband, and businessman. I am proud of the man you have become.

Chuck Michels, we are family and you went above and beyond to provide support during my divorce. Even when I was at my lowest, you encouraged me to look beyond my situation and view myself the ways my father and family saw me. Your compassion and wisdom were pivotal in ushering me along my path to healing.

I feel compelled to mention my friend Pastor Jim Streib and the impact he had on my life over the last thirty years. Although his story was not told in this book, I speak of him often after losing him in 2021. He was a charitable leader of men. Like my father, he observed things in me when I could not see them myself. There was a *Gravity of Up* about him that pulled me along when I was low. When I pass one day, my goal is to be remembered in the same fashion as this amazing man.

I finally made the decision to start this book when I was recovering from surgery in July 2020. It gave me time to reflect, process, and relive the stories that made me who I am today. However, those moments wouldn't have made into this book without the help of Al Fuentes, Chris Dowling, and Alice Sullivan. I'm humbled by your efforts and forever grateful for enabling me to share my story with the world!

To all those who have loved me in my life, I am grateful. I haven't gotten here without each and every one of you.

Now I'm living in the present and relishing what the future holds not only for myself, but for everyone who has read this book and wants to follow this message of healing and pulling others Up. This is a movement of positivity that you are invited to join. I will keep challenging the best people on the planet to keep helping us collectively move forward. Please be on the lookout as soon our gracious team will have products and wellness resources that will reflect exactly where we are all headed—UP!

ABOUT THE AUTHOR

Brent Yates is a serial entrepreneur with over thirty years of experience and success as a business owner, philanthropist, and investor. A leader in the natural gas industry and an Ernst & Young Entrepreneur of the Year nominee, he is now a coveted speaker. Despite having money and prestige, his life journey has been neither smooth nor straightforward. In 2007, he was incapacitated by a mysterious illness, a crumbling marriage, shattered familial relationships, and suicidal thoughts. At his lowest point, God put people, organizations, and resources into his life that came around him and lifted him up from his knees.

This pivotal moment made Brent the man he is today.

He set out on a decades-long pilgrimage to repair his body, mind, and faith. The more love, compassion, and gratefulness he practiced in his day-to-day life, the more abundant his life became. He is inspired to share his success and learned processes with others who are searching for a more balanced and fruitful existence. Brent is involved in many nonprofits and is the founder of RestoreUS, a charity that supports individuals in need both locally and globally with financial and logistical assistance and without the red tape of most organizations.

In 2020, Brent felt God was motivating him through a recurring dream about scaling a seemingly endless mountain. After finally reaching the summit, he clearly heard the words: "Now, what are you going to do?" Accepting the challenge, he penned *The Gravity of Up,* in which he chronicles his arduous passage from brokenness to holistic health. His autobiographical book is a resource not only for business-minded leaders, but anyone looking to overcome their past for a more plentiful future.

MENTAL EXERCISES

By Al Fuentes

I am honored that Brent asked me to close out the book with these mental exercises. Each one of these is based on the very same coaching I gave Brent over the last twelve years. He wanted me to include these exercises because he knows that if you use them as he has, you can reprogram your mindset as well. Even if you don't have the money for a coach, these visualization exercises will make a difference. As long as you do the work consistently, you can experience growth as Brent did in his life. The work begins with an introduction to what visualization is. Then the questions ask you to reflect on your own life story and do the visualizations that you can download for free on www.gravityofup.com/book.

Introduction

Take some time to understand what visualization is. Use the "Beginner's Guide" audio on gravityofup.com/book.

1. Take time to write down at least twenty life victories to start building your positive fuel list. Then sit with them every morning and breathe them in. Feel the success of the moments and see the person that you are in them. (Use the "Positive Fuel" Visualization on gravityofup.com/book.)

2. Create a practice every day for five to fifteen minutes where you breathe in through the nose and out through the mouth to center your body. During that time visualize your day. Create an elevated thought around your actions. See yourself as being more mindful, communicating more clearly, and being more present. Take this as far as you want. (Use the "Preparing Your Day" Visualization on gravityofup.com/book.)

3. Create a "Reset Your Perspective" exercise. To do this, combine your victory list with a visualization. With your eyes closed and breathing properly, see a timeline of your life in your mind as if you are looking at a horizon. See how many things you have accomplished and have

overcome. As you look at your past events, feel how small they feel now compared to where you are today. Then visualize any of today's challenges far out in front of you. See them the same size as past experiences. Realize at this moment that they are not any bigger. Then take deep breaths in to anchor yourself in this reset perspective. (Use the "Reset Your Perspective" visualization on gravityofup.com/book.)

4. How are you motivated to change? Is it only when life gets painful or there is a problem? Look back at your life and see where you have changed. See what has motivated that change. There are only two paths to growing—the path of pain and struggle and the path of abundance and flow. (Use the "Growing Through Abundance and Flow" visualization on gravityofup.com/book.)

5. When you find yourself in a challenging situation, take a look back at all the small choices you made that put you there. See how much they mattered to the overall outcome. Let this exercise put you in a more mindful state as you make choices in everyday life. (Use the "Getting Clarity on the Situation in Front of You" visualization on gravityofup.com/book.)

6. How often do you observe your actions and choices? Take time at the end of the day to reflect on your day and look for moments when you reacted with your ego or humanness. These will usually be tied to one of the more uncomfortable emotions such as impatience, fear, doubt, lack,

worry, or some version of any one of these. (Use the "Observing My Humanness" visualization on gravityofup.com/book.)

7. How often do the negative events outside of you, or even the ones inside of you, affect your energy and bring you down? If you said often, then that would be normal because it typically does that. The challenge I ask you to take up is to find an energy within you through visualization and breath and focus on it every morning. Build it to be strong enough to sustain you even when these negative things happen. Keep in mind this is very challenging, so give yourself some grace. (Use the "Breathing in My Truth" visualization on gravityofup.com/book.)

8. How often is your mind either in the past or the future? Are you looking at the mistakes of the past, or are you worried about the future? First, take a day to observe your thoughts. Keep a tally card to mark each time you are either in the past or future. That night, reflect on how many times you were out of the present. Then the next morning, think about what it looks like to be more present with each part of your day. Write down any notes, then go and live your day, being more present in the moment. (Use the "Being Present" visualization on gravityofup.com/book.)

9. How seriously do you take mental preparation? If you want to be ready for a conversation, meeting, sale, or new stage in life, you have to mentally prepare. Then you don't leave it up to chance.

(Use the "Game Time" visualization on gravity-
ofup.com/book.)

10. Take time to observe your body and how it feels
    when you are stressed. Notice where the stress
    goes. Take time to sit down in a chair and do
    some deep breathing. Focus on that breath, in
    through the nose to that body-specific part.
    When you breathe out, feel that area relax. It may
    feel awkward at first (it was for me), but give it
    some time and see if it will work for you. (Use
    the "Releasing Stress" visualization on gravity-
    ofup.com/book.)

11. Think about how blessed you are to have the
    body you have. What would it be like to celebrate
    it through movement today? You don't have to
    train simply because you're overweight or want
    bigger muscles. Move your body to say thank
    you. How would it feel to train with gratitude
    versus feeling you are not enough? (Use the
    "Body Gratitude" visualization on gravityofup.
    com/book.)

SUGGESTED READING

- *Contagious Generosity: The Key to Continuous Blessing* by B. L. Cameron
- *Good to Great: Why Some Companies Make the Leap... and Others Don't* by Jim C. Collins
- *Rich Dad, Poor Dad* by Robert Kiyosaki
- *The Maxwell Leadership Bible* by John C. Maxwell
- *A New Earth: Awakening to Your Life's Purpose* by Eckhart Tolle

REFERENCE NOTES

1 Coldplay, "Up & Up," track 12 on *A Head Full of Dreams*, Atlantic Records, 2015.
2 Barry L. Cameron, *Contagious Generosity* (CITY: College Press Publishing Co., Inc., 2006).
3 Barry L. Cameron, *Contagious Generosity*.
4 Tim McGraw, "Humble & Kind," track 11 on *Damn Country Music*, Big Machine Label Group, 2015.
5 Tim McGraw, "Humble & Kind."
6 Nellann Young, "Thrifty Preacher Leaves Big Estate," Worldwide Faith News Archive, January 22, 2001, https://archive.wfn.org/2001/01/msg00093.html.